CANADA
Trois Rivieres
St. Peter
Montreal
Utawas R.
Sertigan
L. St. Francis
Lake Champlain
Crown Pt.
Ticonderoga
NEW YORK
VERMONT
NEW HAMPSHIRE
MAIN
Massachusetts Bay
Passamacqudi Bay
Belfast
Penobscot Bay
Casco B.
Portland
York
Jefferys Ledge
Piscataque Hr.
Portsmouth
C. Ann
C. Cod
St. Georges Bank
Bennington
Saratoga
Schenectady
Albany
Boston
MASSACHUSETTS BAY
Providence
Hartford
CONNECTICUT
New haven
RHODE ISLD.
Newport
Marthas Vineyard
Nantucket I.
Nantucket Sheals
Chatham
Sandy P.
The Sound
LONG ISLAND
Staton I.
Sandy Hook
New Inlet
Li. Egg Harbr.
Gr. Egg Harbr.
C. May
Bristol
Trenton
Philadelphia
Newtown
Bethlehem
Easton
Berwick
Muncey
Tyoga R.
Oswego
LAKE ONTARIO
Halifax
Mahon B.
Belfast
Sheals
Marthas Vineyard

LOWER
CANADA
River St. Laurence
R. St. Maurice
Quebec
Chaudiere R.
Trois Rivieres
Sertigan
L. St. Peter
Montreal
L. St. Francis
St. John
Chambly
Lake Champlain
Crown Pt.
Ticonderago
George L.
Saratoga
Mohawks R.
Schenectady
Albany
Hudsons R.
Kingston
Delaware R.
New York
Staton I.
Sandy Hook
Amboy
Trenton
Elizabeth
Burlington
New Inlet
Li. Egg Harbr.
Gr. Egg Harbr.
Salem
VERMONT
Bennington
Windsor
Walpole
NEW HAMPSHIRE
Ports mouth
Piscataqua Hr.
Salisbury
Newbury
Dunstable
MASSACHUSETTS BAY
Boston
Cambridge
Salem
C. Ann
C. Cod
Barnstable Bay
Chatham
Sandy P.
Plymouth
Falmouth
Nantucket I.
Nantucket Sheals
Marthas Vineyard
Newport
RHODE ISLE
Bristol
Providence
CONNECTICUT
Hartford
Enfield
New haven
The Sound
LONG ISLAND
Hampsted
MAIN
Belonging to Massachusetts Bay
Sagadahock R.
Kenebec
Brunswick
Casco
Portland
Wells
York
Casco B.
Jefferys Ledge
St. Georges Bank
Belfast
Penobscot Bay
Mt. Desert
Passamaquady Bay
St. Croix R.
St. Johns R.
S. Anns

NEW ENGLAND
COCKTAILS

AN ELEGANT COLLECTION
OF 100 RECIPES
FROM THE NORTHEAST

MATTHEW REED BAKER

CIDER MILL
PRESS

BOOK
PUBLISHERS

NEW ENGLAND COCKTAILS

ISBN-13: 978-1-64643-459-6
ISBN-10: 1-64643-459-5

This book may be ordered by mail from the publisher. Please include $5.99 for postage and handling. Please support your local bookseller first!

Books published by Cider Mill Press Book Publishers are available at special discounts for bulk purchases in the United States by corporations, institutions, and other organizations. For more information, please contact the publisher.

Cider Mill Press Book Publishers
"Where good books are ready for press"
501 Nelson Place
Nashville, Tennessee 37214
cidermillpress.com

Typography: Farmhand, Avenir, Copperplate, Sackers, Warnock

Photography credits on page 356

Printed in India

23 24 25 26 27 REP 5 4 3 2 1

First Edition

CONTENTS

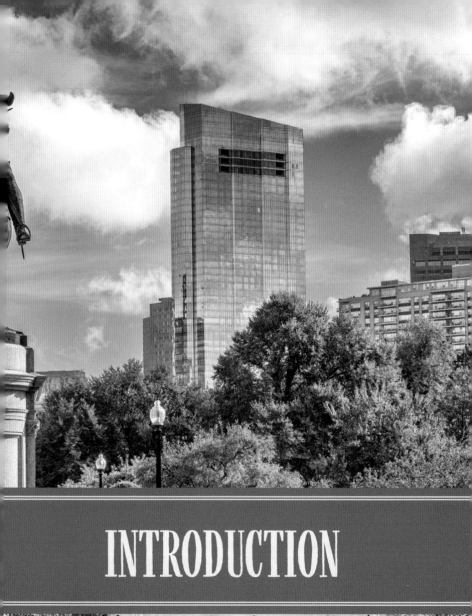

INTRODUCTION

Bully Boy Distillers (see page 300)

WELCOME TO THE UNITED STATES OF NEW ENGLAND

For a remote region tucked far up in the northeasternmost corner of the United States, New England has an outsized role in the country's history as well as an iconic cultural identity. Indeed, the region is small by American standards: its six states add up to a little more than 70,000 square miles, or about the size of North Dakota alone. And despite its well-worn images of wee country villages and quaint family farms, New England can be often densely populated, as it's home to a total of 15 million people.

Of course, New England is not a monolithic entity, but six separate states, each of which plays a different riff on a similar melody.

 **Massachusetts** is the beating heart of the region, not only having the most people and the largest city, Boston, but also being the state that has contributed more than any other to the mystique of New England, whether it's the Pilgrims landing at Plymouth Rock, presidents and financial titans holidaying on Cape Cod or the islands (Martha's Vineyard, Nantucket), or Hollywood actors hamming up the dropped Rs in their faux Boston accents.

Connecticut is the southernmost state and often neglected, as travelers are in a rush to get farther north. It also has the distinction of being considered somehow "less New England" because of its proximity to the region's cultural nemesis, New York City. But its Colonial history, natural wonders, and cultural offerings are as numerous and inviting as any other New England state's, and it has a vibrant cultural center in New Haven and one of the region's most popular scenic towns in Mystic.

Rhode Island is the third state in southern New England and the tiniest in the country. It's dominated by Providence, the political, financial, and quirkily wonderful cultural capital, but it also has some of the best beaches in New England, as well as a beautiful maritime culture, thanks to Narragansett Bay, which almost splits Little Rhody in two.

Vermont is second only to Massachusetts in capturing the imaginations of visitors. It's the land of maple syrup, Ben & Jerry's ice cream, marquee microbrews, and the Green Mountains. It has a reputation for being so cozy and scenic that it's almost too perfect, but it also has a funky vibe as well as cool arts and culture scenes, best exhibited in its largest city, Burlington.

New Hampshire is Vermont's fraternal twin, literally hugging it all along the Connecticut River. From its evocatively gritty and historic cities to the south, to the Lakes Region in the middle, to the White Mountains in the north, the state has dramatically varied terrain, so much of it breathtaking, and while it doesn't market itself as the picture-postcard paradise next door, it certainly could— but with its flinty attitude, it proudly chooses not to.

Caledonia Spirits (see page 340)

**Maine** feels huge by comparison, as it comprises half the land area of all New England. Bordered only by the mountains of New Hampshire to the west, the Atlantic Ocean to the east, and Canada to the north, it certainly feels like a land apart. Indeed, it can feel like an untamed fantasy of rocky coastlines, forests packed with black bears and moose, and a friendly populace who can't imagine living anywhere else. But it also is an agricultural powerhouse as the world's top supplier of lobsters and wild blueberries, and it boasts an internationally lauded foodie city in Portland.

Even if all six states have their own feel and local pride, they do share a common history, one that helped forge the ideas of America, as well as its deep relationship with alcohol that's been there from the very beginning.

PLYMOUTH ROCK

LANDING PLACE OF THE

PILGRIMS

1620

COMMONWEALTH OF MASSACHUSETTS

THE BIRTHPLACE OF AMERICAN HISTORY
AND AMERICAN COCKTAIL HISTORY

Just about every American schoolchild knows the highlights of New England's role in the founding of the United States. At the very least, a basic education teaches them how the Pilgrims landed at Plymouth and celebrated the first Thanksgiving with the Wampanoag people who were already living there. They learn about these earliest American colonies and how the fight for independence from England had its roots here, with such iconic moments as the Boston Tea Party and Paul Revere's ride warning that the British were coming, as well as "the shot heard round the world" on Concord's North Bridge, which kicked off the American Revolution. And throughout US history ever since, New

The famous political protest against England called the Boston Tea Party has long captured the imagination of independent-minded New Englanders.

A late-nineteenth-century depiction of the *Mayflower*

England has been rife with geniuses who have brought the world a wide array of inventions, such as the telephone, the ballpoint pen, vulcanized rubber, basketball, anesthesia, infant formula, Facebook . . . and so on, changing how we experience the world up through today.

And in various ways, New England has changed how we drink. Here are just a handful of the most important examples:

The Colonists first settled permanently on American shores in December 1620, and within three years, they had great success planting apples in Plymouth—much more success than planting vines or grains. What made apples so crucial for the settlers wasn't just that they were food; more importantly, they were used for apple cider. Back in those days, of course, drinking water was a dangerous crapshoot. On the *Mayflower* ride over, the men, women, and children famously drank beer, and once on land and working in the fields, apple cider was both refreshing and safer to drink, and once it started to ferment, it gave them a nice buzz. Soon, apples spread far and wide throughout the colonies. By the watershed year of 1776, Founding Fathers like Benjamin Franklin and John Adams were avid tipplers of the stuff, and it's estimated that one in ten farms in the colonies grew apples. According to cocktail historian Corin Hirsch, New England colonists would then mix the cider with other booze, like combining it with rum to make a Stone Fence, a protococktail if there ever was one. All that being said, we must grudgingly give the Laird family of New Jersey the distinction of distilling the first apple brandy, but it's hard to imagine any of it happening without those enterprising arborists in southeastern Massachusetts.

NEW ENGLAND AND RUM

New England played a much more central role in bringing rum to the world, and this history is deeply complex, with elements of swashbuckling romance but also the most notorious inhumanity. On the one hand, we often hear the heroic folklore of brash Revolutionary privateers raiding British boats and stealing their rum, but on the other, we also need to hear about how rum traveled in Atlantic waters in the first place. Rum itself was created by slaves in the West Indies— the first recorded mention of it is from 1650 in Barbados. By the late 1600s, plenty of it was being produced in new towns like Boston and nearby Medford, where it found popularity as something a bit stronger and warmer to the soul than hard cider. It also became popular with slave traders, so when its use exploded, what is known as the Triangle Trade came into being: slaves would be brought from Africa to the Caribbean, where they were traded for the molasses and sugar

The Martha's Vineyard ferry

produced there; the molasses and sugar would be sent to New England and made into rum; then the rum would be sent to the slave traders in Africa to pay for more slaves. By the time the Declaration of Independence was proclaiming unalienable rights to life, liberty, and the pursuit of happiness, rum was such a major industry in New England that the region boasted some 150 distilleries, with Boston and Newport the epicenters. So even though these very same states popularized rum for the masses—and rum is, of course, a wonderful thing—and even though these very same states were among the first in the nation to abolish slavery, one must always remember that they went hand in hand.

NEW ENGLAND AND ICE

A less controversial but more crucial innovation from New England is commercial ice. Not a spirit, sure, but who can imagine a cocktail without ice, whether served on the rocks or mixed in another crucial and local invention, the Boston shaker (see page 28). Indeed, the first commercial ice harvesting was in Massachusetts, led by "The Ice King of New England," Frederic Tudor. By 1805, he was cutting up and selling ice from frozen ponds all around Boston, even Walden Pond, later of Henry David Thoreau fame. Soon ice harvesting became another unlikely but massive business, with the frozen goods shipped all over the country, as far and wide as New York and New Orleans, where it was put in drinks and early cocktails. Refrigeration and mechanically produced ice would eventually kill off the harvesting of frozen ponds, but only after it began making our alcohol nice and cold.

A street plaque marking the historic Freedom Trail in Boston

NEW ENGLAND AND THE FIRST COCKTAIL BOOK

And then there's the man credited as the father of American mixology, as he not only was a superstar bartender who would travel the country and the world, but was also the author of *The Bar-Tender's Guide: How To Mix Drinks, or the Bon Vivant's Companion*—the first cocktail book ever published in the United States. Jerry Thomas was born in New York State in 1830, but grew up in New Haven, Con-

Baxter State Park, Maine

necticut, and according to local historian Colin M. Caplan, he began his barkeeping life at age 15, working for his brother David at the Park House hotel. A nomadic soul, Thomas would leave at age 19 and try his hand at the Gold Rush out west, but instead he made quite a reputation there for creating unusual libations. His New England connection was not lost, however, as his family stayed in New Haven. Thomas returned in 1852 to help his brothers run a different hotel, while opening a separate bar and casino, where he would serve his California cocktails to New Haveners and Yalies alike. He left for good two years later when his father died, and ran saloons around the country. And though he would gain his ultimate fame with his book and with the popular Manhattan saloon he opened on Broadway, his saga all began on Chapel Street in New Haven.

PROHIBITION IN NEW ENGLAND

On a less convivial note, New England has always had that stubborn streak of Puritanism, even when it comes to the alcohols that it did so much to promote. In fact, the great state of Maine was the first in the country to pass a law prohibiting the sale of alcohol in 1851. It wasn't exactly a success, as people continued to find ways to drink, and the law was so unpopular that it led to Portland's famous Rum Riot four years later. The law was repealed soon after, but by 1885, Maine's identity as a dry state was actually codified into its state constitution. The other New England states also toyed with their own teetotaler statutes (known as "Maine laws" by this point), with varying success. But did that keep New Englanders from drinking? Hardly. In fact, when Prohibition became the law of the country in 1919, as the 18th Amendment of the Constitution, hidden speakeasy bars flourished in all the major cities and even some of the resorts like the Mount Washington Hotel.

And while the most famous rum runners are those who would come out of the Caribbean, they were also prevalent on the New England coast, where they would bring European rum down from Canada.

Even though Prohibition was repealed in 1933, New England states still grapple with "blue laws," which have restricted the times and places for alcohol sales since the late 1700s. For years, you couldn't buy liquor in Connecticut on Sundays, for example, and Massachusetts still outlaws happy hours. Even though these laws are being abandoned more and more each year, they still add to the image of New England as a region that goes to bed early, because the bars have to close early. (But that's okay! People start earlier here too.) And why are these statutes called "blue"? Because the first known laws were printed on blue paper, in New Haven, where Jerry Thomas first started bartending. It's just one of these quirky ironies that come with a place of such long, rich history as New England.

TRAVELING IN NEW ENGLAND TODAY

Tourists flock to New England all year round to explore all of this history and its natural wonders in person. But the region today has complexity as fascinating as those timeworn tales. The contrast between the bucolic idyll and the gritty, bustling urbanity gives New England its buzz, its savor. Indeed, within an hour or two by car you can reach snowcapped mountains or rocky shorelines or sunny beaches or a lovingly restored town that dates back to the Colonial era of the 1600s. But you can also spend days in just one of its many cities, each of which is rich with historical sites, arts and entertainment, and a cultural diversity fostered by immigrants from all over the globe. In New England, you can have a peaceful visit or a vibrant one . . . but best of all, you can combine the two.

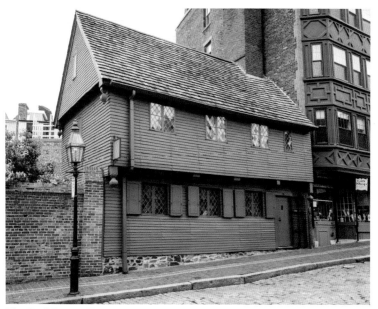

The Paul Revere House in Boston's North End neighborhood

Each state has at least one nationally renowned, buzzy city, packed with top restaurants and bars: Boston in Massachusetts, New Haven in Connecticut, Providence in Rhode Island, Portland in Maine, Portsmouth in New Hampshire, and Burlington in Vermont. Each of these cities is worth days of sightseeing and imbibing. But this list becomes more incomplete every day, as haute cuisine and craft cocktails move into smaller cities and towns and even tiny villages, where the rent is cheaper and where proprietors lean in to make their establishments friendly for locals and desired destinations for outsiders. And even though the region has long had a huge number of acclaimed microbreweries, the population of craft distillers, both in the city and in the country, has been coming on strong, especially since the 2000s.

Woods Hole ferry terminal, Cape Cod, Massachusetts

What these assorted bars, restaurants, and distillers most often have in common is a focus on artisanal quality, environmental sustainability, and supporting their fellow local businesses. The locavore movement is strong here, whether you're talking about farm-to-table cuisine or garden-to-glass spirits. And time and again, these entrepreneurs speak of not only reducing carbon footprints by staying as local as possible, but also of building community with their customers and their colleagues. So while bars and restaurants very often have to close earlier than, say, in New York or Miami, you'll find a much cozier and

less exclusive attitude here, even if bartenders are using the same techniques and better ingredients than in those famously trendsetting burgs.

If you're keen on exploring New England, you'll be surprised at how long it can take to get from place to place for such a small area, which is due to dense traffic in the cities and winding labyrinths of rural backroads. So you may need to take just one route at a time. If you're coming from New York and points south, you can drive up the Connecticut coast, stop in New Haven, then go north through

Vermont

western Massachusetts, up through Vermont to Burlington. Or you could continue east from New Haven along the wetlands of the Connecticut shore to Mystic and then into Rhode Island and up to Cape Cod or Boston. If you're starting your trip in Boston, this hub of New England can be your starting point to the Cape (where you can get a ferry to Martha's Vineyard or Nantucket), Rhode Island, and Connecticut, but you can also head north into New Hampshire or northeast into Maine, where you can get lost for weeks inland or along its 3,500 miles of tidal coastline among its bays and inlets. Whichever route you take, know that this book is merely an overview of New England's many beautiful sights, cultural highlights, and myriad places where you can get a deliciously crafted cocktail made with ingredients that can only be found right where you're drinking it.

Lastly, just remember this one piece of advice: take your time. Sure, there may be many must-see tourist attractions, or a remote distillery that you're trying to reach before it closes. But don't worry if that drive takes too long, and don't feel rushed. New England may not be the most laid-back place on Earth, but it certainly doesn't lend itself to hectic schedules either. The pleasures and wonders of the place are subtle and reveal themselves over time, over those long, winding drives, over those drinks on a porch at your inn, on a streetside patio, or at a picnic spot with a view of the ocean or the mountains. So just take all the time you want and relax with that drink at the end of each day, because there is a world of discovery in New England waiting for you.

HOW TO SET UP A HOME BAR

Lonnie Newburn, always
ready with advice

If the best part of traveling around New England for any cocktail enthusiast is trying new drinks in new places, the most challenging part is making them at home. This is especially true if you are like this author, who has thrown cocktails together for years with only a minimum of knowledge, technique, and proper supplies. For fifteen years, from 2008 to 2023, Bostonians like myself could visit the good folks at the iconic cocktail supply store The Boston Shaker to build a basic set of equipment and ingredients that dramatically helped us amateur mixologists. The Boston Shaker was located in the Davis Square neighborhood of the funky city of Somerville, Massachusetts, just across the river from Boston. It carried everything you needed: a wide range of bar tools, glassware, small-batch bitters, flavored syrups and shrubs, and an extensive but carefully curated selection of cocktail recipe books and histories. In addition to being a one-stop shop, it also offered craft cocktail classes and hosted special events and tastings. It was a fantastic place to begin or end your journey through New England mixology and is sorely missed. However, while it was still going strong, owner Lonnie Newburn gave me an education on how to choose what you need and why you need it, in order to make just about any of the cocktails in this book. Let's follow along as Newburn himself guides you through the essentials.

THE HARDWARE

"When you start with basics," Newburn says, "you need tools that will help you measure appropriate amounts of ingredients precisely. You need tools for the two major techniques of mixing cocktails—shaking and stirring—then the right one for straining the ingredients."

Jigger. There are many different styles, but Newburn recommends a **1 oz. x 2 oz. jigger** that has measurement lines on the inside. "You run into the ½-ounce amounts for spirits, and smaller amounts for flavors," Newburn says, "but you only need one tool."

Shaker. Newburn is adamant that you use a tin-on-tin **Boston shaker**—its standard sizes are composed of an 18 oz. and a 28 oz. tin. "This is still the modern tool for shaking a cocktail, as it's the fastest way to cool a drink or combine ingredients in a fast infusion," Newburn says. "Plus, it's large, so you can make a batch of two to three cocktails." As for the name: "These tins were originally made in South Boston and were sent all over the world, to Paris or England, and

they named it the Boston shaker—that's the lore. It's an American invention." Once you put the ingredients with ice in the larger tin and close it up with the smaller tin, the seal only gets better when the metal contracts from the cold. Not only will it not leak, it's lightweight and the stainless steel won't rust. You use a shaker most often for cocktails that call for citrus or egg white, or if you want a creamy or cloudy consistency that comes from aggressive aeration. (Never shake anything with bubbles, obviously.)

Cobbler. Newburn vastly prefers the Boston shaker, but he also understands the appeal of this multipurpose shaker that comes in three pieces: lid, strainer, and shaker. Newburn acknowledges that the cobbler shakes cocktails well, especially as it breaks up the ice at different angles, but he warns that if the lid fits poorly, it leaks easily. And if the lid fits too well, it's near impossible to take off. "I have customers come into the store in the morning with a cocktail still in it from the night before, and they ask for help opening it," Newburn chuckles. Then he takes out a cobbler he keeps in the storeroom that nobody has been able to open for years. "People have tried different techniques, different oils, but no luck," he says. "This lid is like Excalibur."

Mixing glass. The traditional vessel when a cocktail needs to be stirred, not shaken, is the mixing glass. Newburn says that if you want to keep things simple, you can always stir in a Boston shaker tin—just never stir in a cobbler.

Barspoon. "The barspoon is the chef's knife of the cocktail world," Newburn explains. "You can stir with it from either end—from the spoon end or the rod. You want one with a larger bowl, and you can measure with it too, about ⅛ ounce (less than a teaspoon). The spiral barrel of the spoon not only allows you a better grip and helps you rotate it, but if you're doing a Highball or topping a drink with Champagne or soda, you can pour it down the barrel, so that you don't lose the bubbles." Stirring is for spirit-forward cocktails with darker and

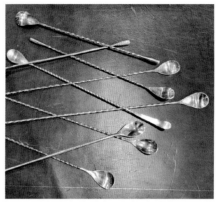 

richer flavors, such as Manhattans and Martinis, so that they are smoother and highlight the stronger flavors.

Strainer. "We carry a wide range of strainers, but the one strainer to rule them all is the **Hawthorne strainer**," Newburn says. "It was invented in Boston in 1895, and it's named after the Hawthorne Restaurant & Lounge that used to be on Avery Street downtown. It's designed to fit the 28 oz. tin in a Boston shaker, but it's universal—it can adjust its coil to fit anything. The Hawthorne allows you to pour the liquid out of the gate between the edge of the tin and the strainer, while the coil holds back any citrus, herbs, or ice. You are guaranteed to get a perfect stream." If you wish to have a secondary strainer, Newburn suggests the **julep strainer,** which is basically a slotted spoon that you hold over a mixing glass.

Muddler. "It's a classic wooden bar tool," Newburn says. "It's the original blender to make a fast infusion in the moment. You can crush water and sugar with it to make simple syrup in a glass. It does a great job with herbs like mint and basil and rosemary, releasing the menthol or essential oils; then you put syrup in there, and you've made a fast-flavored simple syrup. Or you muddle fruits like lime or pineapple for a smash or a bramble, and you infuse the flavor quickly in the spirit."

Garnishing tools. Newburn says a **paring knife** will do for most garnishes, with serration making the job easier. Otherwise, a **wide peeler** makes the classic swath garnishes of lemon and orange peel, while a **twist peeler** will produce the long spiral twists that go on Martinis.

Ice tools. Newburn likes to point out that ice not only completes the drink by chilling it, but it also dilutes the ingredients to achieve the proper balance. He recommends **ice tongs**, so you don't have to taint the drink with your hands. As for making ice, he says you only need **molds for 1-inch and 2-inch cubes**. That being said, a **mold for ice spheres** can come in handy for making Highballs—with no edges, they melt more slowly.

THE GLASSWARE

Nick & Nora glass. This is the original martini glass, which holds about 5 to 6 oz., and like all stemware, it's used so that if you hold the drink by the stem, you don't warm the glass. You can use it for shaken or stirred drinks, just nothing served with ice.

Coupe glass. Newburn says that this is the most common style for drinks served up without ice. He prefers it over the iconic V-shaped martini glass, as its curved sides hold the liquid better without spilling. Even more, Newburn points out, "You can also use it for Champagne or anything with bubbles. A coupe will get you by; you don't need a flute."

Old-fashioned glass. Newburn uses this name to refer to the stemless, cylindrical glass that is also known widely as a **lowball** or a **rocks glass**, and it comes in **single** and **double** sizes. It's a versatile vessel—designed for ice large enough for a 2-inch cube, it also works well for cocktails served neat, without ice.

Collins glass. Also known as the **highball**, drinks in this glass are usually topped with soda or some other sparkler, such as a Rum and Coke or an Aperol Spritz. The design allows you to stack 1-inch cubes and gives you more room for all those bubbles.

THE INGREDIENTS

Newburn can't stress enough that buying the right ingredients is the key to better cocktails. Having a basic setup is not the same as skimping on a better product or using a shortcut in execution. "Just make sure you're getting quality," he says. "There are plenty of spirits that are a good value out here, so you don't need to buy the bottom of the barrel. If you need citrus juice, make it fresh that day. If you're making your own syrups, use them within a week. Make sure your ice is not tainted with other smells from your freezer. And if you can, buy local products, especially here in New England, where we have this whole variety of spirits that are small batch, not industrial, made right here in our backyard."

Spirits. Newburn says that the widest range of cocktails can be made with these basics in your well: vodka, gin, rum, tequila, whiskey, and brandy. When it comes to whiskey, it's best to have a variety, at least including bourbon and rye, while having both light and dark rums is recommended. Lastly, if you like a smoky cocktail, be sure to have some Scotch ready for the whiskey drinks, and to swap mezcal in for tequila.

Liqueurs and fortified wines. "There are tons of modifiers, as these ingredients create the widest range of flavors," Newburn says. "I just recommend that you build your bar cocktail by cocktail. After all, once you buy one, like crème de violette, you'll have it forever, because you only really need it for an Aviation." That being said, you should have both sweet and dry vermouth on hand, and some kind of orange liqueur.

Syrups. Simple syrup is easily the most important ingredient you should always have on hand, but you can just make it yourself by putting a 1:1 ratio of sugar and warm water in a sealed mixing glass and then shaking it until the sugar dissolves. Newburn recommends using only cane or demerara sugar, as white sugar is too bleached, and brown sugar has molasses. Other helpful syrups are flavored with honey, maple, and fruits like raspberry and pineapple, as well as grenadine. Orgeat is a syrup made with almond, sugar, and orange flower water—it's a must for tropical drinks.

Bitters. "Think of bitters as your spice rack for the cocktail world," Newburn says. "Just use a small amount to enhance the flavors. The basic bitters you need are aromatic bitters and citrus bitters—they're like salt and pepper." Traditionally, you use the spiced aromatic bitters for dark spirits, while citrus bitters go with clear spirits, so start here. But now there's been an explosion of bitters, with flavors ranging from floral to cacao to nuts to hot peppers, so think of this as yet another open field for experimentation.

A panoply of bitters

Sodas. "Effervescence is the key for Highballs," Newburn notes, so keep around a selection of club soda, tonic water, cola, and lemon-lime soda, plus ginger ale or ginger beer.

Fruits. "Buy fresh fruit and juice it yourself if possible, and remember that citrus loses its brightness after a day," Newburn says. Use fresh lemons, limes, and oranges, especially since you'll likely use both the juice and the peels. You can get away with cans of pineapple or bottles of cranberry juice.

ONE MORE THING

As a final gift to you, Newburn and his colleague, Elias Eells, sent over these three cocktails that you can add to your repertoire. Each has its roots in New England's long history of making delicious beverages with alcohol and whatever else came to hand.

RASPBERRY LIME RICKEY

This was a traditional highball drink from after the Civil War," write Newburn and Eells. "It was popularized by Colonel Joseph Rickey as a refreshing, effervescent, and originally nonalcoholic drink that was served all over New England. It was once a staple of mom-and-pop corner stores in Maine, Massachusetts, and Vermont; then the Prohibition era added alcohol to the drink, which can now be found reborn in the vacation cocktail culture of New England. The original Raspberry Lime Rickey cocktail called for bourbon as its base spirit, but the drink has been modernized with gin to keep the flavor light, herbal, and refreshing." If you want to make a nonalcoholic version, just add raspberry syrup and a squeeze of lime and top it off with club soda.

GLASSWARE: Highball glass

GARNISH: Raspberries, lime, mint

- 1½ oz. gin
- ¾ oz. raspberry syrup
- ¾ oz. lime juice
- Sparkling water or soda water, to top

1. Add the gin, raspberry syrup, and lime juice to a Boston shaker.

2. Add ice and shake for 10 seconds.

3. Strain over fresh ice into a highball glass.

4. Top with sparkling water or soda water.

5. Garnish with raspberries, lime, and mint.

APPLE BRANDY OLD FASHIONED

Newburn and Eells: "Predating whiskey, in the late 1600s New England's abundant crops of apples led to the creation of apple cider, hard ciders, and ice cider, and eventually the distillation of apple spirits, or apple brandy. Apple brandy was the predominant spirit in the New England colonies and drinking culture. Using this traditional spirit in the classic Old Fashioned recipe creates a rich, fruit-forward nightcap."

GLASSWARE: Old-fashioned glass

GARNISH: Orange twist or apple slices

- 2 oz. Beaver Pond Distillery Apple Brandy
- ½ oz. Vermont maple syrup

- 2 dashes aromatic bitters
- 2 dashes orange bitters

1. Add all of the ingredients to a mixing glass.

2. Add ice and stir for 20 seconds.

3. Strain the cocktail over a large cube into an old-fashioned glass.

4. Garnish with an orange twist or apple slices.

PERIODISTA

Newburn and Eells: "This represents the modern cocktail renaissance of New England, while utilizing a classic New England spirit, Medford rum. Massachusetts has a rich molasses-based rum production history dating back to the 1800s. The Periodista, which means 'journalist' in Spanish, is an example of blending historic and modern ingredients to create a contemporary classic that is unique to New England. This cocktail was created by Joe McGuirk at the restaurant Chez Henri in Cambridge, Massachusetts, circa 2006." You can substitute any molasses-based rum.

ॐ

GLASSWARE: Coupe glass
GARNISH: Lime wheel

- 1½ oz. GrandTen Distilling Medford Rum
- ¾ oz. Cointreau
- ¾ oz. apricot brandy
- ½ oz. lime juice

1. Add all of the ingredients to a Boston shaker.
2. Add ice and shake for 15 seconds.
3. Strain the cocktail neat into a coupe.
4. Garnish with a lime wheel.

SEASONAL COCKTAILS

WINTER:

COCONUT HAMP NOG

PEANUT BUTTER HOT CHOCOLATE

SPRING:

TOMATILLO | PARSLEY

SPIRITED AWAY

SUMMER:

THE CAPE CODDER

THE NEWPORT

BACK PORCH IN JULY

AUTUMN:

AUTUMN LEAVES

CLOUD INVERSION

Along with its varied landscape from the sea to the mountains, New England draws tourists all year round because of its four seasons, which are all postcard perfect in their own ways.

Winter coats the region with snow and ice, creating a wonderland of outdoor activities like skiing and skating, but also a warm aura indoors of fireplaces and cozy gatherings.

Once the dreary mud season passes, spring bursts with wildflowers and bright-green gardens.

Summer is glorious in New England, whether you're hanging out at one of its lengthy beaches, getaway islands, sparkling lakes, or pristine woods.

And lastly, autumn is the famous foliage season, where leaf peepers come from all over the world to see the trees become a breathtaking quilt of oranges, reds, and yellows.

Since the seasons are so distinctly different, bars and restaurants here are dedicated to cocktail menus that change their flavors with the change in the air every three months. Here are nine offerings that will get you through the entire year.

WINTER

COCONUT HAMP NOG

TAMWORTH DISTILLING
TAMWORTH, NEW HAMPSHIRE

What evokes the warmth of a New England hearth and serves almost a meal in itself better than a rich, boozy egg nog? Now you can make a jazzier version, courtesy of Lee Noble, cocktail director of Tamworth Distilling's parent company, Quaker City Mercantile (see page 316). "We use the coconut to make the recipe more exotic," Noble says. "Then we use the maple syrup and mole bitters as a way to add in layers of sweetness and spice, and to dress up an old-fashioned egg nog." This recipe makes four cocktails.

— ❧ —

GLASSWARE: Rocks glass

GARNISH: Grated nutmeg

- 4 large eggs
- 4 teaspoons granulated sugar
- 4 teaspoons maple syrup
- 6 oz. full-fat unsweetened coconut milk

- 6 oz. Tamworth Distilling Old Man of the Mountain Bourbon
- 6 dashes mole bitters

continued

1. Vigorously whisk the eggs, sugar, and maple syrup in a bowl until well incorporated.

2. Slowly add the coconut milk, continuously whisking, followed by the bourbon and bitters.

3. Whisk to completely combine.

4. Garnish with grated nutmeg and serve in a rocks glass over ice, or chill for at least 30 minutes before garnishing and serving straight up.

PEANUT BUTTER HOT CHOCOLATE

SWITCHBACK GRILLE
ROSEBROOK LODGE, BRETTON WOODS SKI AREA, BRETTON WOODS, NEW HAMPSHIRE

The Bretton Woods Ski Area is the largest in New Hampshire, and is just across U.S. Route 302 from the Omni Mount Washington Resort (see page 180). The gleaming Rosebrook Lodge sits where the Skyway Gondola brings you near to the summit of 3,000-foot-high Mount Rosebrook. There, you can get this special treat that will warm you up, whether or not you've been on the slopes all day. It's an extremely simple cocktail, but what does that matter, when it's an extremely wonderful idea?

GLASSWARE: Coffee mug
GARNISH: Whipped cream

- ½ oz. Skrewball Peanut Butter Whiskey
- Hot chocolate, to top

1. Add the whiskey to a coffee mug, then fill the mug with hot chocolate.

2. Garnish with whipped cream.

SPRING

TOMATILLO | PARSLEY

MARCELINO'S BOUTIQUE BAR
I WEST EXCHANGE STREET, PROVIDENCE

For this cocktail featured on Marcelino's spring menu, bar director Refaat Ghostine decided to create an homage to two dishes he cherished growing up in Lebanon: fattoush and tabbouleh. As he puts it, "with each sip, you're transported to the bustling kitchen, the scent of fresh parsley, and the juicy sweetness of tomatoes being lovingly chopped." Ghostine balances the flavors carefully between the vodka infused with parsley—that herb so vital to Mediterranean food—while the fino sherry adds a sophisticated smoothness. And then there are the vegetal flavors. "At the heart lies the star of the garden, clarified tomatillo water," he says.

───────────────── ℬ ─────────────────

GLASSWARE: Rocks glass

GARNISH: Curly parsley

- 40 ml parsley-infused vodka
- 40 ml clarified tomatillo water
- 20 ml clarified cucumber cordial
- 10 ml fino sherry
- 10 ml lemon juice
- 2 dashes chili tincture

1. Add all of the ingredients to a shaker filled with ice.
2. Throw the drink five times for medium dilution, aeration, and to enhance the flavors.
3. Fine-strain the cocktail over ice cubes into a rocks glass, and garnish with parsley.

SPIRITED AWAY

C aleb Landry, the creative director at Blyth & Burrows (see page 98), says that this drink immediately became a huge hit when they introduced it in spring 2019. It's light and floral, and easy for the home bartender to assemble, except for making the horchata out of jasmine rice. But Landry points out that the lactic acid powder is easy to find online or in brewery supply stores, and the extra effort is worth the result. "The batch can be scaled down pretty easily—I'd divide it by four," Landry says. "But it never hurts to have a little extra in the fridge, because it drinks great by itself or with some soda if you're looking for a fun nonalcoholic option."

ॐ

GLASSWARE: Collins glass

GARNISH: Sakura flower or cherry blossom

- 2 oz. soda water
- 2 oz. Jasmine Horchata (see recipe)

- 1½ oz. shochu
- ½ oz. Haku Vodka

1. Pour the soda water into a collins glass to encourage the "fluffing" of the horchata.

2. Whip-shake the other ingredients in a shaker, then strain the mixture into the glass.

3. Garnish with a sakura flower or cherry blossom.

JASMINE HORCHATA: Add 16 cups (4,000 grams) warm water and 4 cups (1,000 grams) jasmine rice to a Cambro container. In a separate cold-brew bag, add the peels of 4 oranges (80 grams) and 8 bags sencha green tea (16 grams). Let the mixtures sit overnight. Remove the tea bags and orange peels, then stir the rice and water together for a short amount of time, until the rice has swollen to the size of BB pellets. Do not overblend. Fine-strain the mixture, then heat it to 140°F and add 2,250 grams Domino sugar, then 100 grams lactic acid, or 1.5% lactic acid by weight.

SUMMER

THE CAPE CODDER

OCEAN SPRAY CRANBERRIES, INC.
LAKEVILLE-MIDDLEBORO, MASSACHUSETTS

Okay, so Ocean Spray is hardly a bar or a restaurant—in fact, it's the farmer-owned cooperative that happens to be the number-one producer of cranberry products in the world. Founded in 1930, it may seem to have grown into an agricultural colossus, but the average size of its member farms is just eighteen acres, and a quarter of them have been handed down over four generations. In southeastern Massachusetts, these tart little red fruits aren't just a primary product but a distinctive part of the culture and the landscape, with cranberry bogs found alongside many a verdant back road. The Cape Codder may be one of the most basic well drinks you can make—and that's because Ocean Spray representatives created it back in the 1940s to sell more cranberry juice in an easily prepared way. It's been an icon of New England summers ever since, and while many bars have jazzed up their own versions, this is the original recipe.

GLASSWARE: Collins glass

- 6 oz. Ocean Spray Cranberry Juice Cocktail, chilled
- 1½ oz. Absolut Vodka
- 1 teaspoon lemon juice

1. Pour all of the ingredients into a collins glass filled with ice and stir

2. Garnish with a fresh cranberry sprig.

THE NEWPORT

FORTY 1° NORTH

NEWPORT, RHODE ISLAND

I f any town knows everything about drinking in the summer, it is Newport, where the scene can be very high-end, very crazy, or both. But if you want an oasis from the crowds that's still lively, head to the Forty 1° North hotel, and if you can get a seat at the Pavilion Bar, you can enjoy a prime waterfront view. Forty 1° North's Kane K. Lewis recommends this refreshing tipple made with cucumber water for the summer.

⁂

GLASSWARE: Collins glass

GARNISH: Cucumber slice

- 2 oz. vodka
- 2 oz. Cucumber Water (see recipe)
- 1 oz. freshly squeezed lemon juice
- ¾ oz. simple syrup

1. Combine all of the ingredients in a shaker and shake hard.

2. Strain the cocktail into a collins glass filled with fresh ice and garnish with a cucumber slice.

CUCUMBER WATER: Place 1 large English-style cucumber and ½ cup water in a blender and blend until the cucumber has completely dissolved, adding more water if necessary. Strain the water through a sieve so there are no cucumber bits left behind.

BACK PORCH IN JULY

VERMONT DISTILLERS
WEST MARLBORO, VERMONT

Dominic Metcalfe runs the Burlington-based tasting room for his father, Ed's, distillery and their full line of spirits (see page 348), and he credits one of his former tasting room employees, Oliver Ash, with this alcoholic take on a Southern sweet tea. Dominic gave the drink its evocative name—as a Grateful Dead fan, he took the phrase from the band's song "Standing on the Moon." If listening to the Dead on a warm day isn't summery enough, Dominic credits Ash with capturing the vibe even better with this advice: "Best enjoyed in a rocking chair, on a porch, surrounded by friends. If these can't be found, an Adirondack chair on a deck with a few acquaintances is an acceptable substitute."

GLASSWARE: Highball glass or mason jar
GARNISH: Lemon slice, mint leaves

- **2 oz. Metcalfe's Vermont Honey Bourbon**
- **1 oz. Metcalfe's Peach Liqueur**
- **Fresh mint leaves, to taste**
- **1 cup unsweetened iced tea, plus more to taste**

1. Place the bourbon, liqueur, and mint at the base of a highball glass or mason jar and muddle well.

2. Add cracked ice and the unsweetened iced tea to taste and stir to combine.

3. Garnish with a lemon slice and fresh mint.

AUTUMN

AUTUMN LEAVES

SPRINGFIELD, MASSACHUSETTS

Dewey's Jazz Lounge is a vital place for its pairing of jazz and cocktails in Western Massachusetts, so it's only appropriate that so many of its drinks are named for musicians or songs. In this case, "Autumn Leaves" is a well-known jazz standard, recorded over many decades by legends like Miles Davis, Duke Ellington, John Coltrane, and Frank Sinatra. Everything about this cocktail suits the season, from the name to the flavors of apple and cinnamon to the mason jar glassware—after all, autumn is when hardy New Englanders start canning their vegetables for the upcoming winter.

GLASSWARE: Mason jar

GARNISH: Apple slice

- Cinnamon, for the rim
- Sugar, for the rim
- 3 oz. apple cider

- 2 oz. Crown Royal Regal Apple Whisky
- ½ oz. vanilla cinnamon simple syrup

1. Rim a mason jar with a mix of cinnamon and sugar.

2. Pour all of the ingredients into the jar over ice and stir to combine.

3. Garnish with an apple slice.

NEW ENGLAND COCKTAILS — 63

CLOUD INVERSION

CALEDONIA SPIRITS

MONTPELIER, VERMONT

S am Nelis is the "Landcrafted Educator" at Caledonia Spirits, which means he's the cocktail guru for the makers of the renowned Barr Hill Gin (see page 340), and he has created here what he calls "a fall-inspired 'tropical' cocktail from Vermont." Roughly inspired by the classic Fog Cutter, this drink uses such northern New England staple flavors as balsam and pumpkin seed, and even adds the unusual northern hardy kiwi, a version of that tropical fruit that can be grown in Vermont—"They look like olives, and are ready to pick in September," says Nelis. As for the name, it captures that awe-inspiring sight of being on the top of a mountain and looking at the bright-blue sky above and the clouds below.

8

GLASSWARE: Pilsner glass

GARNISH: Balsam fir sprig

- 1 oz. Barr Hill Gin
- 1 oz. pear eau-de-vie
- ¼ oz. Smith & Cross Jamaica Rum
- ¾ oz. Vermont Vermouth Zephyr Dry Vermouth
- ¾ oz. lime juice
- ¾ oz. northern hardy kiwi syrup
- ½ oz. pumpkin seed orgeat
- 6 to 7 dashes Angostura bitters, to float
- 4 to 5 dashes orange bitters, to float

1. Add all of the ingredients, except the bitters, to a shaker and shake.

2. Pour the cocktail into a pilsner glass over pebble ice.

3. Float the bitters and garnish with a fresh-picked balsam fir sprig.

otrington o

CONNEC

Waterbury o o M

84

nbury o o ON

CONNECTICUT

FIRE

STIRRED PIÑA COLADA

VAPORS

FORTH & CLYDE

BLACKBERRY BOURBON SMASH

ROSEMARY-CRAN GIMLET

PROFESSOR PLUM

THE MAGICIAN

ESPRESSO MARTINI

KING AZTECA

Connecticut is the gateway between New England and the rest of the country, and the state that links the region to the sprawling New York City metropolitan area. As such, it is often overlooked as a small land of suburbs and highways, but get off those interstates, and you'll find charming towns, stunning beaches, and cities teeming with culture, diversity, and nightlife. New Haven, in particular, has become the cultural capital of the state, thanks to its being the home of Yale University, but also thanks to long-thriving arts and dining scenes, and now it has the boutique hotels to welcome an extended stay. Meanwhile, Mystic and other coastal communities offer all the maritime history and salty atmosphere that anyone would associate with New England. "The Land of Steady Habits" is certainly not only worth a stop on the way north to the other New England states, but also worth a stay in its own right for sightseeing and enjoying its laid-back nightlife.

ORDINARY

990 CHAPEL STREET, NEW HAVEN

When Tim Cabral welcomes you into his snug joint called Ordinary, you leave the bustle of modern-day Chapel Street behind and enter an inviting time capsule of history. All dark, burnished surfaces and warm lighting, with walls boasting ornate woodwork behind the bar and a fireplace that dates back to the 1850s—if you look closely, you will notice that the Freemasons who crafted the place left their marks on their handiwork. Just breathing the air, you can feel like these long, narrow rooms have been host to countless tales before and since. "A lot of storytelling has happened in this space," Cabral says, "and we want to continue it."

To that end, when Cabral and his partners bought the place, he hired local historian Colin M. Caplan to research it, and together they discovered how this corner of Chapel and College streets in New Haven has been a place to get a drink since early Colonial times. A merchant named Stephen Goodyear brewed beer here and built a mansion on this corner in 1646. Just thirteen years later, records show that a proprietor named John Harriman ran a tavern here, called an "ordinary" in those times. Serving locals who worked downtown or by the harbor, which was then much closer, the tavern went through various owners and names throughout the 1700s, even into the American Revolution. General George Washington stopped here on his way to Massachusetts to take charge of the Continental Army, just months after Benedict Arnold knocked on the door and demanded the keys to the powder house to arm the Americans against the British in the Battle of Lexington. (Five years after this heroic moment, Arnold would become the nation's most famous traitor.)

The old "ordinary" was replaced by the 200-room New Haven Hotel, built in 1850 and then considered the most opulent place to stay between New York and Boston. The hotel maintained shops, a restaurant, and the bar at street level, and often served visitors to Yale, which was just across the intersection from its doors. Its most famous visitor was another president, as various accounts say that Abraham Lincoln spent the night there in 1860 while campaigning for the presidency—it was his only visit to the city. And yet this hotel was replaced one more time in 1912, and named the Hotel Taft, after another leader of the United States, Yale alum William Howard Taft. President Taft stayed there when he was a professor at Yale, as did a fourth president, Woodrow Wilson, on his presidential campaign. At the time, it was the tallest building in New Haven, and also the glitziest, thanks to its proximity to Yale and to the neighboring Shubert Theatre, where many classic musicals and shows premiered before moving on to Broadway. As a result, cultural superstars like Humphrey Bogart, Katharine Hepburn, Marlon Brando, and even Albert Einstein stayed at the Taft. Many of these celebrities liked a drink or two, and it's not far-fetched to presume they enjoyed them in the hotel's Tap Room, where you could be sitting now.

For more recent New Haven locals, the bar was long beloved as Richter's, opened in 1982, after the hotel was renovated as an apartment building. Richter Elser was a Yale rowing coach who served beers not just in pints but in long, curvaceous half yards. After twenty years, his bar manager, Dieter von Rabenstein, took over and kept the place the same, until he closed it in 2011. The future of this historic space was in doubt.

Enter Cabral and his partners, Jason and Tom Sobocinski and Mike Farber, who had been variously working in the hospitality and spirits industries for years. "We had heard that a plan had fallen through with this space," Cabral says. "The rumor was that a frozen yogurt chain was going to come in and tear it out. My partners and I are all from here, and we decided that no one was going to ruin this place. So we all decided to renovate it and have a product that would complement it."

Indeed, Cabral himself is a true local, having grown up one town over in West Haven. He started working in restaurants at age 12 as a dishwasher, then at age 16, while earning money at a suburban yacht club, a family friend started teaching him about flavors in food and wine and pairing, and also about the critical importance of customer service. "It's a choice for customers to come and spend their money," he says he was taught, "and we bear a responsibility for how we impact their day." He applied this attitude to decades of bartending and consulting for different restaurants and industry events, so when the opportunity to open Ordinary came around, he had the skill set and experience to match his ethos.

He got rid of televisions in the bar, because he wanted people to connect with the bartenders and with each other. He hired Caplan not only to research the venerable history of the site, but also to write the history, and it appears on the tiled walls in the back room. That relationship also led to the creation of the small New Haven Cocktail Museum which graces the floor-to-ceiling shelves in Ordinary's foyer. He also limited the choice of spirits to producers that he knew personally so that he could vouch for their quality, not just of their products but also of how they do business. But he does so with an eye to educating the customer and helping match their flavor preferences with what may be an unfamiliar brand. And while he loves a good creative cocktail, he never wants the ingredients to be overshadowed. "I'm always of a mindset that simpler is better," he says. "Let a good product showcase itself and be the star of the show."

The result of all this effort has led to some strange and wonderful success. In the oddest scene, Revolutionary War reenactors have staged Benedict Arnold's armament of American troops on the New Haven Green by including that fateful knock on Ordinary's door. Then in 2015, *Condé Nast Traveler* named it one of the 30 greatest bars in the world, but that just made Cabral work harder. "We had news crews showing up at the bar and everything," he says. "I don't do all that well with getting attention, so we had a staff meeting where I thanked everyone, but then we talked about where we could be better, and what I could do better to help them, whether it's learning a new spirit or a new technique." And as a result, he beams when he mentions the "proud-dad moments" of how he hasn't had to hire from outside, as his barbacks have risen to become bartenders over the years. He also has taken on new projects, from partnering with other restaurants in the state—including Gioia, a new Italian restaurant with a rooftop bar and streetside gelato window—to launching New Haven Cocktail Week, involving some forty bars hosting events and featuring industry bigwigs at ticketed seminars, whose revenue was donated to a local women's shelter.

All these elements contribute to Ordinary furthering the remarkable tradition of hospitality, drinks, and history making on this very corner. Being an avid student of this history, Cabral is quite aware of his place in it, as he teaches his staff and clientele about new spirits and flavors and the people who make them. "I was never a great student, but I was good at working, and the restaurant industry embraced me," Cabral says. "And since then, I've always felt that we have to push our education so that we can help enhance the night for customers. There's so much more here than just pouring a drink or giving someone a shot. It's about transferring that history to somebody—things just taste better when there's an association with them."

FIRE

Tim Cabral regularly creates themed cocktail menus at Ordinary, and this one is from his "Elemental" menu. This recipe earns its incendiary name with smoky flavors from chipotle, whiskey, and actual smoke, but balances it with the fruity and floral tang of raspberry and violets.

❧

GLASSWARE: Teapot and teacup

GARNISH: Palo santo smoke

- 1½ oz. McConnell's Irish Whisky
- 1 oz. fresh raspberry tea
- 1 oz. chipotle-maple syrup
- ½ oz. Tempus Fugit Liqueur de Violettes
- ¼ oz. G.E. Massenez Crème de Cassis de Dijon
- 1 pull Liberation Unholy Mole Bitters
- 1 lemon peel
- Freeze-dried raspberry finishing salt, for the rim

1. Add the whiskey, tea, syrup, liqueur, cream, and bitters to a mixing glass and stir to combine.

2. Pour the mixture into a teapot with fresh ice and express the oils from a lemon peel into the cocktail. Garnish with palo santo smoke.

3. Rim a teacup with freeze-dried raspberry finishing salt, upside down on a charred cedar plank. Serve at the table from the teapot into the teacup.

STIRRED PIÑA COLADA

ORDINARY

990 CHAPEL STREET, NEW HAVEN

The Piña Colada is the old standby of many a summer evening, but here Ordinary offers an advanced version that is lighter on the palate, thanks to steeping the coconut in the rum, rather than ladling in heavy coconut cream.

❧

GLASSWARE: Nick & Nora glass

- **Toasted Coconut Maldon Sea Salt, for the rim (see recipe)**
- **1½ oz. coconut-steeped Angostura White Oak**
- **½ oz. González Byass Medium Sherry**

- **¼ oz. Vergnano Maraschino Liqueur**
- **¾ oz. roasted pineapple-lime cordial**

1. Stir all of the ingredients together and serve the cocktail in a Nick & Nora glass rimmed with Toasted Coconut Maldon Sea Salt.

TOASTED COCONUT MALDON SEA SALT: Steep coconut in the rum, then toast it. Once toasted, run the coconut through a spice grinder with the Maldon sea salt.

VAPORS

ORDINARY
990 CHAPEL STREET, NEW HAVEN

T hen there are the completely sui generis cocktails where Ordinary truly shines. Exhibit A: this complex libation that combines smoky mezcal with the earthy sweetness of banana liqueur and honey and the spice from bitters. The chai tea vapor bubble is just the crown on an already majestic drink.

— ✂ —

GLASSWARE: Coupe glass

GARNISH: Atomized chai tea vapor bubble

- 1 oz. Rayu Mezcal
- ¾ oz. Amaro Montenegro
- ¾ oz. Tempus Fugit Crème de Banane
- ¾ oz. lime juice
- ¼ oz. honey
- 1 pull clove-infused ginger bitters

1. Add all of the ingredients to a cocktail shaker with ice.

2. Shake, then double-strain the cocktail into a coupe.

3. Finish with an atomized chai tea vapor bubble.

FORTH & CLYDE

116 CROWN
116 CROWN STREET, NEW HAVEN

Decades ago, Crown Street was once an unpleasantly quiet street after dark in downtown New Haven, but in the years since it has exploded as the Elm City's main street for clubs, restaurants, and cocktail meccas like the one residing at #116. Owner John Clark-Ginnetti is such a scholar of cocktail history that he teaches a seminar on cocktail culture and history at nearby Yale University. And here, he shares perhaps his restaurant's most enduring cocktail, which deftly balances the bitter, sweet, and sour with a touch of heat.

ॐ

GLASSWARE: Martini glass, chilled

- **Honey, as needed**
- **Red chili flakes, to taste**
- **1 oz. Hendrick's Gin**
- **1 oz. Maker's Mark Bourbon**
- **1 oz. St-Germain Elderflower Liqueur**
- **1 oz. fresh-squeezed lime juice**

1. Pour a nickel-sized quantity of honey into a cocktail shaker.
2. Add red chili flakes to taste (the tip of a butter knife is perfect for one drink).
3. Add the remaining ingredients and stir until the honey dissolves.
4. Add as much ice as you can fit into the shaker, then shake for 18 seconds.
5. Strain the cocktail into a chilled martini glass.

BAR

If there's one bar that has done the most over the years to make Crown Street in New Haven a nightlife destination, it's BAR. It opened in 1991, with a front lounge with huge windows that open up to the sidewalk on warm days, and a large back room that was home to local bands and dance nights. The vibe was invitingly hip but not exclusive, and it became both a destination for visitors and a favorite watering hole and hangout for locals.

Then in 1996, BAR dared to open up an adjoining brick-oven pizzeria and microbrewery, called the Brü Room, serving thin-crust pies, to compete in New Haven of all places. Known as one of the most unique and venerable pizza cities—thanks to the world-renowned brick-oven pizzeria trinity of Pepe's, Sally's, and Modern Apizza—New Haven and its citizens are also known for being stubborn pizza snobs. If the dough doesn't have the right chew and the right char on the bottom, it's no good, and the ingredients must not just be high quality but also must have the perfect balance in relation to the thinness of the crust. Thankfully, the pizza here meets those criteria, and has the added bonus of being served both in the Brü Room and right there at the bar in BAR itself.

BAR's bar manager, Sean Gavaghan, has worked here since 2019, when he already had a starry New Haven cocktail pedigree, having kicked off his bartending career at 116 Crown (see page 78) and then serving as one of the opening bartenders for Ordinary (see page 70). But his current employer's pedigree in local nightlife history is not lost on him: "Owner Frank Patrick has curated such a cool culture here, starting in 1991. By morning, we are a craft brewery; for lunch, we are cranking out some of New Haven's favorite pizza; by 6 p.m., we are a cocktail bar; and by 10 p.m., we are a jamming nightclub featuring some of the Northeast's most prominent DJs. BAR is such a local staple, and I am beyond grateful to have a set of keys to this building."

BLACKBERRY BOURBON SMASH

BAR

254 CROWN STREET, NEW HAVEN

On warm evenings when the sun sets late in the day, BAR opens up its streetside windows and the outside patio fills up with laid-back revelers. And it's hard to imagine a better drink for watching nightlife traffic pass by than this refreshing but powerful blackberry smash.

※

GLASSWARE: Rocks glass

GARNISH: Fresh mint, skewered blackberries, lemon wheel

- 2 oz. Old Forester 86 Proof Straight Bourbon Whiskey
- 1 oz. lemon juice
- 1 oz. mint cane syrup
- ½ oz. blackberry puree

1. Add all of the ingredients to a cocktail shaker with ice.
2. Shake, then strain the cocktail over fresh ice into a rocks glass.
3. Garnish with fresh mint, skewered blackberries, and a lemon wheel.

ROSEMARY-CRAN GIMLET

BAR
254 CROWN STREET, NEW HAVEN

This simple but sublime concoction is the perfect beverage to consume in BAR's complex but chic interior. Note of caution: you may find yourself downing plenty of these easy-drinking beauties.

❧

GLASSWARE: Coupe glass
GARNISH: Orchid, rosemary sprig

- 1½ oz. Monkey 47 Schwarzwald Dry Gin
- ¾ oz. lime juice
- ¾ oz. rosemary-cranberry syrup

1. Add all of the ingredients to a cocktail shaker with ice.

2. Shake, then double-strain the cocktail into a coupe.

3. Garnish with an orchid and rosemary sprig.

PROFESSOR PLUM

At first, Simsbury comes across as a pleasant suburb midway between Connecticut's capital city, Hartford, and Springfield, Massachusetts—so pleasant, in fact, that *Money* magazine once named it one of the 10 best places to live in the United States. But it's a bit more than just a nice town: settled in the 1670s, it boasts a historic downtown, the summer home of the Hartford Symphony Orchestra at Simsbury Meadows Performing Arts Center, and a bustling trade in fall foliage tours. Simsbury is also home to Millwright's, a cozy restaurant and tavern that comes with waterfall views and this heartwarming, complex cocktail developed by its acclaimed lead bartender, Jamie Oakes.

GLASSWARE: Rocks glass

GARNISH: Expressed orange peel

- 2 oz. Smoked Plum–Infused Evan Williams Bourbon (see recipe)
- ½ oz. Amaro delle Sirene
- ½ oz. Brown Sugar Syrup (see recipe)
- Dash Scrappy's Cardamom Bitters
- Dash orange bitters

1. Combine all of the ingredients in a mixing glass and stir.

2. Strain the cocktail into a rocks glass over ice.

3. Express an orange peel over the drink and discard.

SMOKED PLUM–INFUSED EVAN WILLIAMS BOURBON: Place 1¼ cups peeled and diced black plums in a bowl with a lid and use a smoking gun to fill the container with smoke. Seal the container and let it sit for 10 minutes. Add the smoked plums to 1 liter Evan Williams Bourbon in a vacuum-sealed bag or large mason jar. Sous vide at 110°F for 15 minutes, then strain out the plums. (If you do not have a sous vide, combine the plums with bourbon the day before and let the infusion sit overnight.)

BROWN SUGAR SYRUP: Stir 2 cups light brown sugar in 1 cup hot water until the sugar dissolves.

THE MAGICIAN

CONSPIRACY
350 MAIN STREET, MIDDLETOWN

Middletown is a small city situated on the west bank of the Connecticut River, and it's also known as the home of the lovely Wesleyan University. Located downtown, right between the flowing waters and the halls of academia, is Conspiracy, a small, evocative joint inspired by the pre-Prohibition cocktail scene. Just pull a comfortable, tufted stool up to the ornate bar that dominates the space, and wash down some savory small plates with an elaborately unique drink, courtesy of husband-and-wife owners Mark and Jen Sabo. Mark explains that The Magician was inspired by South American chicha de jora, a lightly fermented corn drink—one whose flavors are both tropical and touched with a hint of autumn. And as for the name, Mark says, it came from their annual "tarot card" menu, where they make cocktails named after the Major Arcana cards.

GLASSWARE: Double rocks glass
GARNISH: Dehydrated corn husk

- 1 oz. pineapple rum
- ½ oz. reposado tequila
- ½ oz. John D. Taylor's Velvet Falernum Liqueur
- 1 teaspoon Amaro Tosolini
- 1 teaspoon Amaro Dell'erborista
- 2 dashes Bittermens Buckspice Ginger bitters
- ½ oz. lemon juice
- ¾ oz. Cornbread Syrup (see recipe)

1. Add all of the ingredients to a cocktail shaker with ice.

2. Shake, then strain the cocktail into a double rocks glass with ice.

3. Garnish with a dehydrated corn husk.

CORNBREAD SYRUP: Add 155 grams cornbread to a container, then boil 300 ml water. Once the water is boiling, pour it over the cornbread. Allow the mixture to cool, then blend the mixture for 1 minute. Strain the liquid through cheesecloth. Measure it, then add cane sugar in a 1:1 ratio and heat until the sugar is incorporated.

MATCH

98 WASHINGTON STREET, SOUTH NORWALK

Located just four towns in from the New York border, South Norwalk (or SoNo, for short) has long been a popular outpost for professionals working in the Big Apple or in the nearby corporate town of Stamford. The bar scene may be compact, but it's lively, and it's highlighted by Match, a restaurant that combines industrial chic with an old-school vibe. Helmed by chef-owner Matt Storch, a Food Network veteran, the food menu is ever changing, while the drink menu boasts classics with a Mexican twist, thanks to the influence of bar manager Jimmy Ortiz.

ESPRESSO MARTINI

MATCH

98 WASHINGTON STREET, SOUTH NORWALK

In a riff on the classic, bar manager Jimmy Ortiz says he added Licor 43 "for a hint of citrus warmth that really elevates an already great cocktail." This Spanish liqueur is commonly used in the Mexican Carajillo, where it is added to espresso and ice. "This is a nod to my Mexican heritage," Ortiz says. "I wanted to bring just a bit of home into this welcoming community."

GLASSWARE: Coupe glass

GARNISH: 3 espresso beans

- 2 oz. vanilla vodka
- 2 oz. Kahlúa
- 2 oz. Licor 43
- 2 oz. cold espresso

1. Add all of the ingredients to a cocktail shaker with ice.

2. Shake, then pour the cocktail into an 8½ oz. coupe.

3. Garnish with the espresso beans.

KING AZTECA

MATCH

98 WASHINGTON STREET, SOUTH NORWALK

I come from Puebla City, Mexico, located in the burning heart of the former Aztec Empire," says bar manager Jimmy Ortiz. And so he created this fiery concoction by centering it around Ancho Reyes Original, a liqueur made in his hometown using ancho chiles, a dried form of the famous poblano peppers that come from his region. "When thinking about how to best represent myself in a cocktail, I looked no further than this delicious liqueur," Ortiz says. "And with the subtle heat it imbues, it warms the heart of any Aztec warrior enjoying it!"

∞

GLASSWARE: Rocks glass

GARNISH: Lime twist

- 2 oz. silver tequila
- ½ oz. green Chartreuse
- ½ oz. lemon juice
- ½ oz. lime juice
- ½ oz. simple syrup
- ¼ oz. Ancho Reyes Original
- Tajìn, for the rim

1. Add all of the ingredients to a cocktail shaker with ice.

2. Shake, then strain the cocktail over ice into a rocks glass rimmed with Tajìn.

3. Garnish with a lime twist.

MAINE

SHIP, CAPTAIN, CREW

LUMBERSEXUAL

ALGORITHM OF THE NIGHT

COUCH SURFER

HUNTING GROUND

TURMERIC AND TEQUILA

CHAMOMILE CITRUS COLLINS

"ON ANOTHER LEVEL" OYSTER SHOOTER

Maine is by far the largest and most overwhelming state in New England—it takes longer than five hours to drive up the whole coast (that's if you're just breezing through on the highway)—and another five-plus to drive up north to the very top border with Canada. In between all these points are countless villages and sparkling lakes, astonishing seascapes, endless forests, rolling hills, and welcoming farms. You can hike up Mount Katahdin in Baxter State Park or Cadillac Mountain in Acadia National Park, or you can ski down the slopes of Sunday River and Sugarloaf. Best of all, so many of these small towns and cities have newly refurbished general stores and sublime farm-to-table restaurants, led by Portland. By now, it's no secret that Portland is one of the country's premier cities for food and drink—*Bon Appétit* magazine even named it Restaurant City of the Year in 2018—no small recognition for a place boasting just 70,000 people. But however hip its current chefs and cocktail gurus may be, they all have a strong sense of their city's long maritime history, thanks to the old brick buildings, narrow cobblestone streets, and working wharfs. It all means that instead of just driving, you'll be stopping everywhere, and that makes Maine a place you'll travel through not for hours but for a lifetime.

SHIP, CAPTAIN, CREW

BLYTH & BURROWS
26 EXCHANGE STREET, PORTLAND

The craft cocktail bar Blyth & Burrows is named after two ship commanders who fought on opposite sides in the War of 1812. The British commander Blyth and the American commander Burrows were both killed by cannon fire, and their bodies brought to Portland, where they were buried in Eastern Cemetery. At this cozy bar, creative director Caleb Landry offers this appropriately named take on a house-smoked Old Fashioned, but one with deeper flavors. If you do not have access to a smoking receptacle, remove the water from the build, and instead stir the cocktail over ice like any other Old Fashioned.

— ∞ —

GLASSWARE: Rocks glass

- 1½ oz. Dandelion Bourbon (see recipe)
- ¼ oz. Smith & Cross Jamaica Rum
- ¼ oz. Clément Première Canne Rum
- ¼ oz. Amontillado
- ¼ oz. Montenegro
- ¼ oz. Lemongrass 2:1 (see recipe)
- ¼ oz. water
- 1 barspoon Spruce Tip Tincture (see recipe)

1. Combine all of the ingredients in a smoking bottle.

2. Serve in a rocks glass.

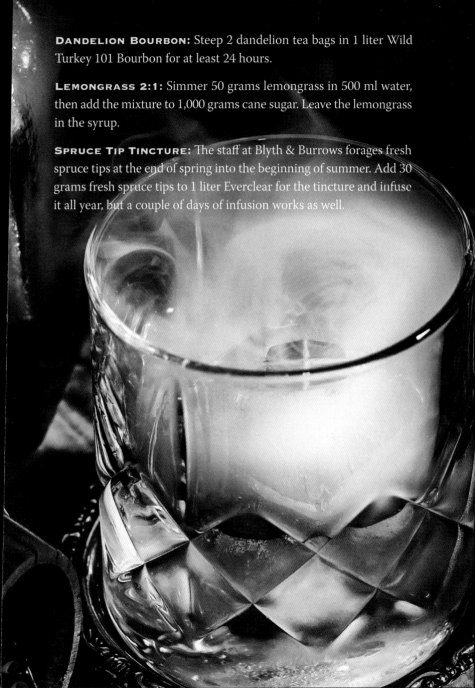

DANDELION BOURBON: Steep 2 dandelion tea bags in 1 liter Wild Turkey 101 Bourbon for at least 24 hours.

LEMONGRASS 2:1: Simmer 50 grams lemongrass in 500 ml water, then add the mixture to 1,000 grams cane sugar. Leave the lemongrass in the syrup.

SPRUCE TIP TINCTURE: The staff at Blyth & Burrows forages fresh spruce tips at the end of spring into the beginning of summer. Add 30 grams fresh spruce tips to 1 liter Everclear for the tincture and infuse it all year, but a couple of days of infusion works as well.

LUMBERSEXUAL

VENA'S FIZZ HOUSE
867 CONGRESS STREET, PORTLAND

Portland is not only a marquee place to eat and drink, but also to shop, especially for artisanal and arcane goods, and the great thing about Vena's is that it houses all of these activities under one roof. Established in 2013 by Steve and Johanna Corman, it began as a mixology shop that also had a bar specializing in old-fashioned, all-natural fizz sodas and mocktails. The year 2015 brought the arrival of a liquor license and hence a craft cocktail menu that focuses on obscure, nostalgic ingredients like bitters, shrubs, tonics, and even vinegary switchels. Today the store offers a full range of bitters and syrups, barware and glassware, and cocktail infusion kits where mason jars house the ingredients—just add spirits. All these specialty items are available for shipping at Vena's online retail shop, but if you can make it to Portland, you can have their humorously titled signature cocktail in person.

ↂ

GLASSWARE: Lowball glass
GARNISH: Lemon slice, fresh rosemary

- 1½ oz. gin
- ½ oz. Vena's Maine Pine Syrup
- ½ oz. lemon juice
- ¼ oz. tonic syrup
- 4 dashes Vena's Maine Pine Bitters
- Seltzer water, as needed

1. Mix all of the ingredients together in a lowball glass with ice.

2. Stir, then spritz with seltzer.

3. Garnish with a lemon slice and rosemary. For an added botanical boost, add 2 more dashes Vena's Wormwood Tincture.

ALGORITHM OF THE NIGHT

BRAMHALL

769 CONGRESS STREET, PORTLAND

Congress Street is Portland's main drag, coursing westward from the East End and its views of Casco Bay, all through downtown, and out to Interstate 295 and the Fore River. As it passes through the sophisticated West End neighborhood, a doorway at Number 769 leads down into a brick-and-stone speakeasy. Lit with candles, subtle sconces, and streaks of light coming through stained-glass windows, it can feel like another time and another place. But it certainly serves a modern array of comfort food and bar snacks, as well as this drink from Bramhall's Jason Rosemeyer. Rosemeyer wanted to combine the flavors of hazelnut and banana, and he found that infusing the noisette liqueur Frangelico with actual bananas worked better than using a separate banana liqueur, while the allspice bitters toned down the sweetness but kept the complexity. The end result, Rosemeyer says, is that "it tastes like a banana bread Manhattan—super rich and decadent on the palate, with a long dry finish."

&⃝

GLASSWARE: Rocks glass

GARNISH: Dehydrated banana

- 2 oz. Ezra Brooks Straight Rye Whiskey
- 1 oz. Banana-Washed Frangelico (see recipe)
- Dash Dale DeGroff's Pimento Aromatic Bitters

1. Add all of the ingredients to a mixing glass with ice.

2. Stir, then pour the cocktail over a big rock in a rocks glass, and garnish with a dehydrated banana.

BANANA-WASHED FRANGELICO: Bramhall does a sous vide water bath for the infusion. For every liter of Frangelico, cut up 3 bananas and throw in the skin. Set the temperature at 135°F, sous vide for 2 hours, then give the mixture an ice bath. Strain and bottle once the mixture is cool.

COUCH SURFER

MAGNUS ON WATER
12 WATER STREET, BIDDEFORD

While Portland has been earning accolades for years as the best restaurant city in the United States, the small city of Biddeford has undergone an impressive revitalization and is now a mini gastronomic hub of its own, just 20 miles southwest of its bigger sibling. With many bars and restaurants gathered in its compact downtown, you can't go wrong, but you can certainly go right with Magnus on Water and its intensely creative cocktail program. Witness the Couch Surfer, bar director Brian Catapang's take on the classic Margarita—topped with a house-made "sea foam," it's as much a sculpture as it is a beverage. "The drink itself is meant to mimic the feeling of getting hit in the face with a breaking wave," Catapang says. "The taste of the breaking whitewater—the foam—is salty, airy, and sour. It's a total shock to the senses, but then you get the refreshing, bright, and smooth base of the ocean, which is the Margarita base." On an ever-changing menu, Catapang says, this is the one that is never taken off.

⮘

GLASSWARE: Lowball glass
GARNISH: Sea Foam (see recipe)

- 1 oz. Camarena Silver Tequila
- 1 oz. Banhez Mezcal
- ¼ oz. Pierre Ferrand Dry Curaçao

- ½ oz. fresh lime juice
- ¼ oz. fresh lemon juice
- ¼ oz. 1:1 simple syrup

1. Add all of the ingredients to a mixing glass and combine.

2. Strain the cocktail into a lowball glass, then garnish with the Sea Foam.

SEA FOAM: Pour 500 ml fresh pineapple juice, 100 ml egg white, 2 oz. Ancho Reyes Verde Chile Poblano Liqueur, 2 teaspoons Maldon sea salt, and ½ teaspoon citric acid into an iSi whipper container and charge with two NO_2 cartridges. Shake vigorously in between charges.

HUNTING GROUND

THE VIEW AT 16 BAY VIEW
16 BAY VIEW STREET, CAMDEN

Located roughly eighty miles both from Portland to the south and Bar Harbor to the north, Camden is the picture-perfect harbor town of Midcoast Maine, and thus has become a choice destination for summer visitors arriving by car or by yacht. And right in the middle of it is 16 Bay View, a twenty-one-room boutique hotel that seamlessly fits a modern aesthetic into an old brick industrial building. But you don't have to be a guest to enjoy drinks at the rooftop bar called The View, which offers 2,000 square feet of alfresco eating and drinking space with a panorama encompassing Camden Hills State Park, the harbor filled with old schooners and new powerboats, and Curtis Island providing the gateway to the rest of Penobscot Bay. On a warm day with a light breeze, it's a spectacular place to drink this light and breezy beverage from food and beverage director Kerry McCormick.

GLASSWARE: Collins glass
GARNISH: Pink orchid, lemon wheel

- 2 oz. Barr Hill Gin
- ½ oz. lemon
- ½ oz. butterfly pea flower simple syrup
- Fever-Tree Soda Water, to top

1. Add all of the ingredients to a shaker and shake.

2. Pour the cocktail into a collins glass with ice.

3. Top with soda water and stir.

4. Garnish with a pink orchid and lemon wheel.

TURMERIC AND TEQUILA

On the side of the harbor where U.S. Route 1 becomes the main street through the town center is where most of the restaurants and shops reside in this delightfully strollable town. And yet, there is only one restaurant where you can get an ideal view of it, and that's from the other side of the harbor, which is dominated by Lyman-Morse, the famed builder of custom powered and sailing yachts. Thankfully, located within Lyman-Morse's marina is Salt Wharf, a sleek box of a building that is all glass windows and open-air patios. Its golden vistas pair nicely with a menu of raw bar small plates, creative seafood entrees, and even osetra caviar served with house chips. And all of it can be washed down with standards like a Dark & Stormy, or with this funky and refreshing vegetal cocktail from bar manager Meghan Werby.

ꙮ

GLASSWARE: Rocks glass

GARNISH: Dehydrated orange, dehydrated lime, pineapple frond

- 2 oz. blanco tequila

- ¼ oz. fresh lemon juice

- ½ oz. fresh orange juice

- 1½ oz. Turmeric Juice Blend (see recipe)

- ¼ oz. agave nectar

- Salt, for the rim

- Freshly cracked black pepper, for the rim

1. Add all of the ingredients to a shaker and shake.

2. Pour the ingredients into a rocks glass rimmed with a mix of salt and freshly cracked black pepper. Garnish with a dehydrated orange, dehydrated lime, and pineapple frond.

3. Torch the orange until nicely charred.

TURMERIC JUICE BLEND: Use a juicer to combine 2 large carrots, 1 red apple, 1 slice (1½-inch-thick) freshly skinned pineapple, and 6 to 7 (3- to 4-inch) pieces fresh turmeric. The juice remains fresh for 5 days, and can be frozen for later use.

CHAMOMILE CITRUS COLLINS

SIDE STREET CAFE
49 RODICK STREET, BAR HARBOR

As the one large town on Mount Desert Island, home to Acadia National Park, Bar Harbor is one of Maine's most bustling vacation destinations during the summer. Hotels, restaurants, and bars are packed as visitors fill the streets looking at the views of the islands out in Frenchman Bay, or looking for someplace fun to get a meal and some good drinks. Just off Main Street, on a narrow side street, is the aptly named Side Street Cafe, where you can enjoy convivial crowds and good grub on the patio. And you can also enjoy what the bar is serving, such as this Chamomile Citrus Collins from bar manager Jasmine Burne. This drink is bright and refreshing, with the delicate florals of the chamomile and the herbaceous tones of the Lillet Blanc invigorated with the juniper of the gin and the tartness of lemon. "Summer in Maine is short and sweet," Burne says, "and this is as close as we've gotten to getting a beautiful New England summer day in a glass."

GLASSWARE: Pint glass or mason jar

GARNISH: Lemon slice

- 2 oz. Chamomile-Infused Dry Gin (see recipe)
- 1 oz. Lillet Blanc
- 1 oz. fresh lemon juice

- ½ oz. simple syrup or agave nectar
- 3 oz. soda water

1. Combine all of the ingredients, except for the soda water, in a shaker and shake with ice.

2. Pour the cocktail into a 16 oz. pint glass and top with the soda water.

3. Garnish with a lemon slice.

CHAMOMILE-INFUSED DRY GIN: Pour 2 cups (16 oz.) dry gin into a sealable container, such as a glass jar. Add 2 chamomile tea bags. Let the infusion steep for 24 hours before removing the tea bags.

"ON ANOTHER LEVEL" OYSTER SHOOTER

THE LOFT RAW BAR & SEAFOOD GRILL
53 MAIN STREET, BAR HARBOR

When in a seaside town in Maine during the summer, the number-one activity on your list should be eating seafood. The ocean's bounty extends far beyond lobster. Here in Bar Harbor, The Loft can fill any yearning for mollusks, crustaceans, or fish, complete with various seafood towers, crudos, pokes, ceviches, and even a "seacuterie" of various types of smoked fish. And The Loft stays focused on hyperlocal sourcing, with all of its oysters coming from farms within a ten-mile radius of the restaurant. Speaking of oysters, The Loft's Christopher Kemna offers this blend of oyster shooter and Bloody Mary, named after their pride in their menu, but also for its second-floor location at Bayside Landing that offers great views of downtown and Frenchman Bay.

❧

GLASSWARE: Cocktail glass
GARNISH: Lemon slice

- 1 oz. Deep Eddy Vodka
- 2 oz. Bloody Mary Mix (see recipe)
- 1 shucked local oyster

1. Dry-shake the vodka and Bloody Mary Mix without ice.

2. Pour the cocktail over ice into a cocktail glass, then top with the oyster and garnish with a lemon slice.

BLOODY MARY MIX: Combine tomato juice, celery salt, sriracha, Old Bay, horseradish, and Worcestershire sauce to taste.

MASSACHUSETTS

THE BOHEMIAN

THREADING THE NEEDLE

FEAR FACTOR

LEAVE IT TO ME

SNAKES & RAINBOWS

CLOSING ARGUMENTS

NEGRONI BERGAMOTTO

MODEL-T

DUMBLEDORE'S OFFICE

BRAZILIAN FIZZY

WHITE RABBIT

PINK PEPPERCORN SANGRIA

THE DOCKSIDE

CROWN SPRITZ

PERMISSION GRANTED

BILLIE'S HOLIDAY

PEAR MARTINI

The Commonwealth of Massachusetts is the very heart of New England—geographically, historically, and culturally. Not only does it lie in the center of the region, separating the northern states from the southern ones, but it is also the only state of the six that extends from the western border with New York State all the way to the Atlantic Ocean in the east. Of course, this is the land where the United States really began, from the Pilgrims landing at Plymouth Rock to the Boston Tea Party, and from Paul Revere's ride to the battles of Lexington and Concord. Any visitor to the state is eager to see all these historical sites, but the present day offers many eclectic delights as well. The villages in the western Berkshires, the college towns in the Connecticut River Valley, and the eastern coasts of rocky Cape Ann and beachy Cape Cod all feel like different worlds. And then there is Boston, New England's largest city by far: it's a bustling, diverse conurbation of five million people that offers some of the country's best arts and music scenes, as well as a seemingly unlimited assortment of places to relax with or splurge on top-shelf food and drink. Any trip to New England usually starts here, and with good reason.

DRINK

348 CONGRESS STREET, BOSTON

Decades ago, Boston was often derided—by New Yorkers, at least—for being a culinary backwater, a foodie landscape dominated by clam chowder, steak tips, and dive bars serving a shot and a beer. That time is ancient history, and one of the primary movers who has transformed the city and its standards for dining is Barbara Lynch. She was raised in the 1970s in some of South Boston's toughest housing projects, and, remarkably, her entire formal culinary education was a home economics class in high school. But with fierce drive and inestimable talent, Lynch worked her way up through restaurants, eventually running the kitchens at some of celebrity chef Todd English's top restaurants. By 1998, she opened her own place, the fine-dining mecca No. 9 Park, right on Boston Common, which was named Best New Restaurant by *Food & Wine*. From there, she opened several more top-rated restaurants and won a handful of James Beard Awards, including one in 2014 for "Outstanding Restaurateur." She was just the second woman to win this category.

Amid all this excellence, Lynch also embarked on a very different project, opening Drink in 2008. Dedicated to the art of the craft cocktail, she applied the same high standards of concept, design, ingredients, and execution that were her trademarks elsewhere. The first thing one will always notice upon entering Drink is the bar itself, a long, continuous wooden counter that snakes throughout the space to seat a lot of people and creates six different corners and nooks for hanging out. Meanwhile, there is no clutter, as the bottles are hidden out of sight—all a customer watches, as Lynch has put it, is "people chipping ice and cutting herbs . . . everything is custom-made." As an example of Drink's influence, many of Drink's bartending alumni have gone on to open their own lauded bars, like Sam Treadway of Backbar (see page 139).

Despite its haute-cuisine founder and top-shelf pedigree, Drink is warm and unpretentious to visit. The venue sits below street level, with windows letting light in at the top, while simple bulbs and brick walls pay homage to the Fort Point neighborhood's old industrial history. The total effect is a place with a chic, warm intimacy, and the pleasure of a cocktail being crafted with care from scratch, just for you.

THE BOHEMIAN

DRINK
348 CONGRESS STREET, BOSTON

According to general manager Roberto Cibrian Stockbridge, this drink was invented by Misty Kalkofen, one of Drink's superstar alumni, who went on to open the renowned Brick & Mortar in Cambridge and coauthored the cocktail book *Drinking Like Ladies*. Stockbridge says that this tart, floral, easy-drinking cocktail has been on the menu for more than fifteen years, and is easily the drink that Drink pours most—no mean feat, considering how many impressive ones have been created in its wake. Plus, for the home bartender, it's a versatile recipe: "You can change the gin for tequila, rum, or vodka, and it will always taste delicious," Stockbridge says.

꙰

GLASSWARE: Coupe glass
GARNISH: Edible flower

- 1 oz. Citadelle Gin
- 1 oz. grapefruit juice
- 1 oz. St-Germain Elderflower Liqueur
- ¼ oz. lime juice
- 3 dashes Peychaud's bitters

1. Combine all of the ingredients in a shaker and shake.

2. Strain the cocktail into a coupe.

3. Garnish with a fresh edible flower.

THREADING THE NEEDLE

DRINK

348 CONGRESS STREET, BOSTON

This invention is much more recent, created by Stockbridge out of a desire to have cocktails that utilize the smoky flavor of mezcal without being overpowered by it. He found the smoky notes work well with the subtle bitterness and floral sweetness of the other ingredients, especially one particular spice: "The saffron goes so well with the smoke," Stockbridge says, "that many times when I serve this cocktail, people become amazed to find that they start liking mezcal!"

&

GLASSWARE: Nick & Nora glass
GARNISH: Dehydrated lime wheel, fresh mint

- 1 oz. Banhez Mezcal
- ¾ oz. Aperol
- ¾ oz. lemon juice
- ¾ oz. Apologue Saffron
- ¼ oz. honey syrup

1. Combine all of the ingredients in a shaker and shake.

2. Pour the cocktail into a Nick & Nora glass.

3. Garnish with a dehydrated lime wheel and fresh mint.

FEAR FACTOR

PARLA

230 HANOVER STREET, BOSTON

Surrounded by Italian restaurants on the main drag of Boston's North End, Parla is a Mediterranean restaurant whose interior and cuisine manage a glowing balance between rustic charm and urban cool. And so it is with their cocktails. As general manager Patrick Panageas explains, he was inspired by his Greek and Portuguese heritage to create this "exploration of olive oil as it pertains to the cocktail world." The shrub may be extra work, but he says it adds just the touch of acidity to bring this nutty and creamy drink up to the next level.

GLASSWARE: Coupe glass, chilled

GARNISH: Amargo Chuncho bitters, furikake, dried cricket

- 1½ oz. Del Maguey Crema de Mezcal
- ½ oz. Licor 43
- ½ oz. lemon juice
- ¼ oz. extra virgin olive oil
- ¼ oz. honey simple syrup (1:1)
- ¼ oz. Roasted Beet Shrub (see recipe)
- 1 egg white

1. Dry-shake all of the ingredients together in a shaker, then add ice and shake again.

2. Double-strain the cocktail into a chilled coupe.

3. Garnish with 1 spray Amargo Chuncho bitters, plus a light dusting of furikake and a dried cricket to top.

ROASTED BEET SHRUB: Preheat the oven to 375°F. Put 4 whole beets in a deep-dish baking pan, fill one-third of the pan with cold water, and cover it with tin foil. Place the pan with the beets in the oven for 35 minutes. Take out the pan and remove the tin foil. After allowing the beets to cool, peel them and chop them into 1-inch cubes (be sure to wear gloves to avoid staining your hands). Add enough granulated sugar to coat every surface of the beets. Place the beets in the refrigerator for 6 to 8 hours. Strain through a fine-mesh chinois. Add white distilled vinegar at a 2:1 ratio of yielded sugar juice to vinegar. Label and store in the refrigerator for up to 3 weeks.

THE STREET BAR

1 NEWBURY STREET, BOSTON

The Newbury Boston may have just re-opened under that name in 2021, but it's been the premier luxury hotel in Boston since 1927. Back when it was built, it was one of the first Ritz-Carlton hotels in the United States, and it was still called "the Old Ritz" even after Taj Hotels bought it in 2007, renaming it Taj Boston but keeping all the finery and maintaining the same quality of service. But once the Taj moved on in 2019, Highgate Hotels purchased it, completed an extensive restoration, worked with Major Food Group to create dining and cocktail programs, and renamed it most appropriately after the street where it resides. After all, this location has always been one of the poshest addresses in the city. It sits across the street from the verdant Public Garden, famous for its swan boats that glide in its central lagoon. And it welcomes you to Newbury Street, Boston's deluxe retail thorough-fare where you can find the likes of Chanel, Burberry, Bvlgari, and Armani, as well as many art galleries, salons, and independent boutiques.

LEAVE IT TO ME (NO. 2)

THE STREET BAR
I NEWBURY STREET, BOSTON

You can spend a day just being a flaneur and people watching on Newbury Street, then you can finish the day at the hotel with two choices: either have the afternoon tea, which has been served at this location for more than ninety years, or seat yourself at the burnished Street Bar and order up this velvety variation on the classic Clover Club cocktail.

— ∞ —

GLASSWARE: Coupe glass
GARNISH: 3 raspberries

- 2 oz. Grey Goose Vodka
- ¾ oz. Raspberry Simple Syrup (see recipe)
- ¾ oz. lemon juice
- ¼ oz. Lazzaroni Maraschino
- 1 oz. egg white

1. Combine all of the ingredients in a shaker.

2. Seal the shaker tins and dry-shake for 15 seconds to emulsify the ingredients.

3. Shake with ice for 10 to 15 seconds.

4. Double-strain the cocktail with a Hawthorne strainer and a fine-mesh strainer into a coupe. Garnish with the raspberries.

RASPBERRY SIMPLE SYRUP: Combine 500 grams raspberries and 500 grams white sugar in a deep saucepan, then gently press the mixture with the back of a fork. Let it stand for 15 minutes, then add 500 grams water. Set a stove burner to medium heat and bring the mixture to just below a boil. Remove it from heat and let it cool for 30 minutes. Strain the syrup through a fine-mesh strainer or cheesecloth. Store in the refrigerator for up to 3 weeks.

HECATE

PUBLIC ALLEY 443,
BOSTON

In the spring of 2022, Hecate arrived on the Boston cocktail scene with a swirl of dark ambience and an air of bewitching intrigue, only suitable for a hot spot named after the Greek goddess of magic and sorcery. Located downstairs from Krasi, the popular Greek restaurant and wine bar, you enter through a black door in an alley, and after passing through a vestibule called "The Threshold," you enter an intimate netherworld of deep, dusky hues and deeply complex drinks, creatively inspired by mysticism.

HECATE

PUBLIC ALLEY 443, BOSTON

F or each cocktail on our menu, we tie in a story that aligns with some form of magic or mysticism from around the world," says beverage director Lou Charbonneau. "In this case, we are referencing Haitian Vodun, better known to the world as voodoo. Ayida-Weddo is a loa [divine spirit] of fertility, rainbows, wind, water, fire, and snakes. Ayida-Weddo is known as the Rainbow Serpent. This cocktail plays on the symbolism of Vodun practices using ritual ingredients, Haitian rum, and the favorite style of soft drink from the country. The oyster itself is known as an aphrodisiac and symbolizes fertility—the vessel being a desire demon also plays to that end." Though it may take some effort to make it, you'll find it worth mastering this magic potion.

— ⮾ —

GLASSWARE: "Desire demon" tiki mug
GARNISH: Oyster shell filled with Palo Santo and Vetiver Granita
(see recipe); palo santo, dried sage, mini tarot card

- 1½ oz. Boukman Botanical Rhum
- 1½ oz. Palo Santo and Vetiver Verjus Cordial (see recipe)
- ½ oz. lime juice
- ½ oz. Tropi-Cola Sparkling Cola Champagne Soda

1. Combine all of the ingredients, except the soda, in a shaker and shake.

2. Pour the cocktail over cubed ice into a "desire demon" tiki mug, then add crushed ice on top. Top with the soda.

3. Garnish with an oyster shell filled with Palo Santo and Vetiver Granita, palo santo, dried sage, and a mini tarot card.

PALO SANTO AND VETIVER VERJUS CORDIAL: Combine 10 grams palo santo; 10 grams vetiver root, cut into pieces with scissors; 500 grams sugar; and 500 grams white verjus and sous vide at 203°F (95°C) for 14 hours. This recipe yields 1 liter. Store the cordial in the refrigerator for up to 2 weeks.

PALO SANTO AND VETIVER GRANITA: Combine a 3:1 ratio of ice to Palo Santo and Vetiver Verjus Cordial (see recipe) in a blender. Blend until smooth. Store the granita in the freezer, scraping occasionally with a fork as it is freezing to get the desired consistency.

SARMA

Just across the river from Boston and adjacent to Cambridge, Somerville is the most densely populated municipality in New England and one of the densest in the country, with some 80,000 souls packed into just four square miles. Since the late 1980s, it has been transformed from a working-class city best known as the erstwhile headquarters of Irish gangsters to a bohemian haven for artists, musicians, and writers. Even with the inevitability of gentrification, it's still a remarkably diverse place—the public school district boasts an array of students coming from families speaking more than fifty different languages. And in its different neighborhoods, often centered around public squares, you can find a remarkably diverse selection of acclaimed restaurants. Behold Sarma: it's a hip and cozy, modern Mediterranean neighborhood joint in Gilman Square, helmed by chef-owner Cassie Piuma, who has been nominated for a James Beard Award almost every year since 2015. In addition to the bold, entrancing mezze plates on offer, Sarma also presents intriguing flavors in elegantly conceived cocktails.

CLOSING ARGUMENTS

SARMA

249 PEARL STREET, SOMERVILLE

Sarma beverage director Cameron Brown presents Closing Arguments as a Greek interpretation of a Last Word, the Prohibition-era gin cocktail. Instead of that drink's use of green or yellow Chartreuse, Brown uses mastic liqueur, derived from the sap of mastic trees growing on the Aegean island of Chios, which gives the drink an "herbaceous punchiness," as Brown puts it. Then with the balance provided by St. Germain's fruity elderflower tones and a dash of Peychaud's anise flavor, "it drinks extremely smoothly with vibrant floral, pine, and citrus qualities," Brown says. "It's perfect for year-round sipping."

— ଠ —

GLASSWARE: Coupe glass, chilled

GARNISH: Grapefruit coin, expressed

- ¾ oz. Bully Boy Sarma Gin
- ¾ oz. Roots Mastic Liqueur
- ¾ oz. St Germain Elderflower Liqueur
- ¾ oz. freshly squeezed lime juice
- Dash Peychaud's bitters

1. Add all of the ingredients to a mixing tin, add ice, and shake vigorously for 10 seconds, until chilled.

2. Double-strain the cocktail through a Hawthorne strainer and a conical strainer into a chilled coupe.

3. Garnish with an expressed grapefruit coin.

NEGRONI BERGAMOTTO

SARMA

249 PEARL STREET, SOMERVILLE

Brown credits one of his colleagues, Pat Harmon, with this beverage, and he says that Negroni variations are a mainstay at the bar, because they're fun to play with and can be combined in unlimited ways to pair with the food they serve. "We decided to take inspiration from our kitchen team, as we usually do," Brown says, "so we workshopped a delicious Negroni riff around the bergamot orange—an Italian bitter citrus fruit." They use a whole ounce of the Italicus Rosolio di Bergamotto to bring that citrus flavor forward, paired with the smokiness of the mezcal. Brown praises the specific dry vermouth they've chosen here for its citrus and herbal notes, while the Luxardo Bitter Bianco "brings the cocktail full circle with its up-front, bright bitterness."

GLASSWARE: Double old-fashioned glass, chilled

GARNISH: Orange twist, expressed

- 1 oz. Italicus Rosolio di Bergamotto
- ¾ oz. Yzaguirre Reserva Dry Vermouth
- ¾ oz. Luxardo Bitter Bianco
- ½ oz. Mezcal Unión Joven

1. Add all of the ingredients to a mixing glass, then add ice and stir for 10 seconds, until chilled.

2. Strain the cocktail over fresh ice into a chilled double old-fashioned glass.

3. Garnish with an expressed orange twist.

BACKBAR

Despite its consistent rating as one of the Boston area's best bars since it opened in 2011, Backbar is certainly a challenge to find. First, you need to navigate the warren of avenues that gets you to Union Square in Somerville, which has become one of the Boston area's most au courant neighborhoods for bars and restaurants. Then you need to find Sanborn Court, a nondescript alley that looks more like a parking lot. Once there, just look for the barely marked red door. Push it open, and you walk down long, dark hallways daubed with murals celebrating pop culture touchstones like Garfield, *Jaws*, and R2-D2. You know you're in the right place when you see the parody of the album cover for Pink Floyd's *The Dark Side of the Moon*: a martini glass takes the place of the iconic prism. Open one more door, and you're in a comfy, postindustrial space with high ceilings and concrete floors, and any number of delicious-looking bottles behind the bar.

This is Backbar, the beloved hangout that is treasured locally—it's a regular winner of *Boston* magazine's Best of Boston awards—but also has been lauded worldwide, including in 2021, when *Time Out* named it one of the twenty-eight coolest bars in the world. And it's the brainchild of industry veteran Sam Treadway, a native of Weston in Boston's western suburbs, who started bartending during college summers and worked a circuitous path to his own legendary spot where he can be as creative as he wants, essentially coming up with his own libation laboratory and cocktail menu.

And yet the first big-name drinking establishment that employed him was as far away from that boutique standard as possible. Over those summers during college he worked at Cheers, the big bar based on the legendary Boston-based sitcom, located in the heavily touristed Faneuil Hall. He parlayed that famous name into a regular job back in Northfield, Minnesota, where he was a student at Carleton College. At the Tavern of Northfield, he learned what it meant to have a place where regulars could just show up and feel at home while nursing a favorite drink. "I had Benny the Tattoo Guy, and Steve who would come in on the way home for a beer and a shot," Treadway says with affection. "I felt the vibe of hanging out and being the host of the party." He did that for the rest of college, and even though his hospitality career took many twists and turns after that, the crucial need for this hangout vibe would come into use many years later.

But first, he worked in the bar at an upscale Seattle hotel, got homesick, then returned to Boston, where he worked as a barback at the beloved Eastern Standard bar near Fenway Park. He started at this entry-level position because he found out that being a basic bartender is not the same thing as crafting custom and classic cocktails. Soon enough, in 2008, he found that the chef-restaurateur Barbara Lynch was going to open her marquee cocktail bar, Drink (see page 118), and he wanted in, so he signed up as a barback there too. But that bar's bad fortune with initial construction delays turned out to be good fortune for Treadway: "We had multiple weeks of training thanks to the delays, so every day we were mock bartending, studying, and learning, and I proved myself worthy. In fact, the day before we opened, they said you're not a barback now, you're a bartender." He worked there for two years, becoming one of the venue's star class of bartenders and creating a fan base of regulars. Despite a brief sojourn at a job he couldn't turn down—being a head bartender at a luxury hotel in Hawaii—his status as a Drink alum was crucial to him creating Backbar.

The year was 2011, and husband-and-wife duo Tse Wei Lim and Diana Kudayarova were launching Journeyman in Union Square, a restaurant that would earn wide acclaim for its culinary innovation. Lim and Kudayarova were regulars at Drink and admired Treadway's skills with a cocktail, and they had emailed him in Waikiki about opening his own bar as an adjunct to Journeyman. When his Hawaii gig ended, he jumped at the chance and soon was picking out the site of the bar in this odd space that was once a garage for a Ford dealership, built in the 1920s. The one thing missing was the name. Lim and Kudayarova chose Backbar, because it was the back of the restaurant. Treadway didn't love the name, but their other suggestion was Barback, so the former barback went along with the first choice, and he's never looked back, despite an evolution of the bar's image.

"It was going to be a fancy-shmancy cocktail bar, very serious, where we take reservations and wear a coat and tie," Treadway says, "but the place evolved into a neighborhood bar with good drinks, and now it's one with serious, intense nerdy undertones, and we lean into that!"

Indeed, any pretentious vibe has long been replaced by a fun, goofy geekery, with printed cocktail menus themed after Star Wars, Harry Potter, Shakespeare, Ursula K. Le Guin, Disney, or Black Panther . . . indeed, you're more likely to see Hogwarts or Wakanda referenced in a cocktail theme than a labored riff on an obscure botanical. In fact, Treadway's menus are so lovingly designed and printed—whether it's a menagerie of drinks named after bird species, or a cocktail trip around the solar system—they feel like collectible objects in their own right.

"I took inspiration from other bars around the globe—like Trick Dog in San Francisco, or the Artesian in London—that are doing more and more involved menus with a cohesive thought process that the guest could follow along with. These menus have set us apart, being a bit more thoughtful in what we're doing. We just have a lot of fun with different themes and engaging people, while having a wide variety of drinks in each theme, because everyone has a different palate. I feel like I've created a pretty cool space that a lot of different guests and bartenders have called home. When I started, I found bartending to be easy, which is rare, because a lot of people get stressed about it and the long hours. But I just felt that if I was learning about cocktail histories and the different cultures around alcohol, then it's fun, especially if I'm taking care of people. Alcohol is supposed to be fun, so you might as well present it as a good time."

MODEL-T

BACKBAR

7 SANBORN COURT, SOMERVILLE

Backbar's signature drink is the Model-T, named in honor of its host building, which was built as a Ford dealership in 1921. "When we first opened back in 2011, we wanted a twist on a Manhattan that was simple and unique," Treadway says. "The clove aroma is a spike of flavor that pairs well with the oaky notes of the double-aged bourbon."

GLASSWARE: Nick & Nora glass, chilled

GARNISH: Cherry

- 1¾ oz. Jim Beam Black Bourbon
- ¾ oz. Carpano Antica Formula Vermouth
- ½ oz. Yellow Chartreuse
- Dash Angostura bitters
- Clove-infused rum, for the rinse

1. Add all of the ingredients to a mixing glass and stir with ice.

2. Strain the cocktail into a chilled Nick & Nora glass that has been rinsed with clove-infused rum.

3. Garnish with a cherry.

DUMBLEDORE'S OFFICE

BACKBAR
7 SANBORN COURT, SOMERVILLE

Named after the head wizard's luminous lair in the Harry Potter series, this drink is Backbar's most popular of all time. Treadway takes visible pleasure in telling the story: "Back in 2018, we had a World Map menu with cocktails inspired by different places all over the world. We decided to be cheeky and have a couple of mythical places on there, so this drink was located at Hogwarts on the map. If you know the Harry Potter books, then you might remember that one of the passwords to get past the gargoyle outside of Dumbledore's office was 'lemon drop.' He was a fan of the little candies, but we thought about making a riff on the classic Lemon Drop Martini. So this is tart and refreshing but magically complex, with elderflower playing well with passion fruit and ginger. And the garnish is an ode to Fawkes, the phoenix who lived in the office."

GLASSWARE: Coupe glass, chilled

GARNISH: Lemon ash

- 1 oz. Bombay Sapphire Gin
- ½ oz. St Germain Elderflower Liqueur
- ½ oz. limoncello
- ½ oz. fresh lemon juice
- ¼ oz. passion fruit syrup
- ¼ oz. ginger syrup
- 1 egg white

1. Add all of the ingredients to a shaker and dry-shake without ice.
2. Shake with ice.
3. Strain the cocktail into a chilled coupe.
4. Garnish with lemon ash.

MUQUECA

1008 CAMBRIDGE STREET, CAMBRIDGE

Right next door to Somerville is its sister city, Cambridge, best known as the home of Harvard University and the Massachusetts Institute of Technology (MIT), as well as Kendall Square, a sprawling area that has one of the highest concentrations of technological innovation in the country. But beyond the high-tech and higher education is a vibrant, bustling city with many eclectic communities. Thanks to its centuries as a home for Portuguese fishermen, the Boston area has long been a destination for Lusophone immigrants, and as a result is one of the big three cities for Brazilians in America, alongside New York and Miami. You can get a taste of Brazilian culture just about anywhere in the urban area, but the best is right near hip Inman Square, thanks to this veteran Brazilian restaurant.

MUQUECA
1008 CAMBRIDGE STREET, CAMBRIDGE

Along with several variations on its namesake seafood stew, Muqueca also offers the sausage-and-bean stew feijoada, various grilled meats, and veggie options like a lasagna made with plantains. Even better, you can get many a refreshing cocktail to brighten these rich meals: Caipirinhas abound, of course, but Muqueca's Roberta Aranha also recommends this sparkler. "On a hot Bostonian summer day," she says, "the Brazilian Fizzy was conceived. We wanted to create a drink that would represent Espírito Santo, the state in Brazil where the owner of Muqueca is from, and to give you the feeling of being on the beach. Pineapple was the clear choice; mint to add freshness; and everything is more fun with bubbles."

— ❦ —

GLASSWARE: Rocks glass
GARNISH: Pineapple slice, mint sprig

- 1¼ oz. vodka
- 3 hand-ripped mint leaves
- 2 oz. pineapple juice
- Dry sparkling wine, to top

1. Add the vodka, mint, and pineapple juice to a shaker with ice.
2. Shake well.
3. Strain the cocktail into a rocks glass filled with ice and garnish with a pineapple slice and a mint sprig.
4. Top with a dry sparkling wine.

PAGU

Located mere blocks from the international scientific mecca that is MIT, surrounded by international innovators packing the Kendall Square district, Pagu fits in with its innovative international cuisine that blends pan-Asian and Spanish cuisines. Founded by chef-owner Tracy Chang, Pagu has been feted by local and national press, and was a James Beard semifinalist in 2023, thanks to its eclectic menu featuring jamón ibérico, fried oysters in squid-ink bao buns, black cod croquetas, and suckling pig fit for a party of six. What makes Chang and Pagu even more exceptional is how the chef has used her stature to feed people who don't come to her restaurant, by cofounding organizations like Project Restore Us and Off Their Plate to provide supplies and meals for food-insecure families across Greater Boston. As of this writing, these organizations have provided more than 800,000 pounds of food to more than 8,000 working families.

You can feel the community spirit in the restaurant itself, despite its sleek design. The vibe is casual and friendly, and the food feels homey, especially Pagu's trademark Guchi's Midnight Ramen, an addictive umami bomb of noodles and broth that will send you home sleepy and satisfied. And even though the cocktails can be complex and combine unusual flavors, they always feel fresh and welcoming with every sip. Bar manager Andy Bechtol explains how he works this trick with the two luscious libations that follow.

WHITE RABBIT

The White Rabbit cocktail is an amalgamation of all the ways I've been taught to approach a cocktail in the last five years," Andy Bechtol says. "I gained a strong appreciation for Clément Rhum Blanc when I worked at a rum-heavy bar, and I learned a lot about how to efficiently batch a cocktail for speed from my time in New York City. What developed was this blend of funky rum and yogurt flavors, a lime-acid cordial that saved us from having to shake a drink (while bringing the ticket time down to about 45 seconds), and ultimately the creamiest clarified Daiquiri. It's one of those drinks that, when you break it down, is truly very simple—and I think that's why we all love it so much."

&

GLASSWARE: Rocks glass
GARNISH: Baby's breath flowers

- 1¼ oz. Yogurt Rhum (see recipe)
- ¾ oz. Dolin Blanc Vermouth
- ½ oz. Lime-Acid Cordial (see recipe)

continued

1. In a mixing glass, stir all of the ingredients over ice.

2. Strain the cocktail into a rocks glass over a large ice block.

3. Garnish with baby's breath flowers.

YOGURT RHUM: Using a whisk, thoroughly mix together 750 ml Clèment Rhum Blanc and 262 grams plain yogurt. Add 94 grams lemon juice and whisk again. Leave the mixture out at room temperature for 30 minutes. Strain through a chinois and coffee filter until clear.

LIME-ACID CORDIAL: Mix 500 grams sugar, 500 grams water, 16 grams citric acid, and 10 grams malic acid together and bring to a simmer, or use hot water to dissolve the ingredients.

PINK PEPPERCORN SANGRIA

PAGU

310 MASSACHUSETTS AVENUE, CAMBRIDGE

Pagu's Pink Peppercorn Sangria is a very floral spin on a classic White Sangria," Andy Bechtol says. "We use frozen strawberries to infuse Marie Brizard Triple Sec, and pairing it with Matchbook Distilling's Day Trip Strawberry Amaro makes for a really good strawberry flavor. I've always been a sucker for pink peppercorn, and I know if any of my past bartender friends read this they'll be laughing in agreement, so naturally it had to find its way into the drink. A few touches of Peychaud's bitters added the color I wanted but also the tiniest little wisp of anisette alongside the elderflower tonic. It's obvious how nontraditional this recipe is, but it's delicious!"

GLASSWARE: Wineglass

GARNISH: Pink peppercorns

- 4 oz. white wine blend
- 1½ oz. Strawberry-Infused Triple Sec (see recipe)
- 1 oz. Fever-Tree Elderflower Tonic Water
- ¾ oz. Pink Peppercorn– Infused Vodka (see recipe)
- ½ oz. Matchbook Distilling Day Trip Strawberry Amaro
- 3 dashes Peychaud's bitters

1. Mix all of the ingredients together and serve in a wineglass, over ice, with strawberry slices and lemon wheels.

2. Garnish the top with pink peppercorns.

PINK PEPPERCORN–INFUSED VODKA: Add 75 grams pink peppercorns into a 750 ml bottle of Ketel One Vodka. Let it sit and infuse for 48 hours. Strain before using.

STRAWBERRY-INFUSED TRIPLE SEC: Add 1,132 grams frozen strawberries into 3 liters of Marie Brizard Triple Sec. Let it sit and infuse for 24 hours.

AQUA BAR

Perhaps the most famous vacation destination in New England, Cape Cod is a flat curlicue of a peninsula, connected to the mainland by just the Sagamore and Bourne bridges. Where it extends sixty-five miles into the Atlantic Ocean, it's home to the Kennedy dynasty's summer compound, a national seashore with miles of pristine beaches, and scenic towns and sites that are packed all summer. And at the very final tip of the peninsula is quirky Provincetown, with funky shops, a thriving LGBTQ community, and clubs and restaurants galore. The waterfront also has vast views of Cape Cod Bay, and thanks to Aqua Bar, you can sip and sun with the sea extending out in front of you.

THE DOCKSIDE

AQUA BAR

207 COMMERCIAL STREET, PROVINCETOWN

General manager and head bartender Ken Ross offers this aptly named cocktail, inspired by the winter months he spends down south. "I love a good, traditional Old Fashioned cocktail," he says, "but there are so many delicious rums in Puerto Rico and the Caribbean. I find a slight similarity between some of the not-so-sweet rums and some of the higher-end ryes and bourbons, so I experimented, and this was the result."

GLASSWARE: Lowball glass

GARNISH: Orange peel, dark cherry

- 1½ oz. Goslings Black Seal Rum
- ¾ oz. Captain Morgan Original Spiced Rum
- ¼ oz. simple syrup
- 3 dashes orange bitters

1. Fill a lowball glass with cracked ice.

2. Add all of the ingredients and stir.

3. Garnish with an orange peel and a dark cherry, such as Luxardo.

CROWN SPRITZ

CROWN & ANCHOR
247 COMMERCIAL STREET, PROVINCETOWN

This restaurant-bar–entertainment complex on Provincetown's main drag, Commercial Street, has a slogan that sums it up perfectly: "On a summer's night, the Crown & Anchor can't be missed. In fact, it can't be ignored." Indeed, this building with its trademark portico and tower was built to be noticed, as its first incarnation back in the nineteenth century was as an event hall, bowling alley, and saloon. Nowadays, it's a massive epicenter of LGBTQ nightlife and arts, with cabaret drag queens out front welcoming in passersby, who will find inside a boutique hotel, a restaurant, performance venues, a gallery, and six distinctly different bars. Indeed, the whole colorful place and the town itself can feel a world away from the drab mainland, and so co-owner Jonathan Hawkins offers this tart twist on an Aperol Spritz as "a little Cape Cod with a splash of Italy."

GLASSWARE: Wineglass

GARNISH: Orange twist, mint leaves

- 1½ oz. Aperol
- Prosecco, to top
- Splash cranberry juice
- 2 mint leaves

1. Fill a wineglass with ice, then add the Aperol.

2. Top off with prosecco and add a splash of the cranberry juice.

3. Add a couple of mint leaves and garnish with a thick-cut orange twist.

PERMISSION GRANTED

THE PROPRIETORS
9 INDIA STREET, NANTUCKET

Thirty miles off the southern coast of Cape Cod lies the island of Nantucket, whose Wampanoag name means "The Faraway Land." If the crowded cobblestone streets hem you in too much, you can always rent a bike and cycle all over the island, as it is only fourteen miles long and three and a half miles wide. In the main town, there are endless options to sate the appetite you've just earned. And you can hardly do better than this gastronomic hub from restaurateurs Michael and Orla LaScola. The Proprietors is the home of a gorgeous bar running the full length of the cozy wood-beamed first floor, and thanks to managing partner Anna Worgess, you can settle in there with this fruity, silky cocktail.

❧

GLASSWARE: Highball glass

GARNISH: Freshly grated nutmeg

- 2 oz. WhistlePig PiggyBack 100 Proof Bourbon

- ¾ oz. Apologue Persimmon

- ¾ oz. Yakami Orchards "Marugoto Shibori" Yuzu Juice

- ¼ oz. freshly squeezed lemon juice

- 1 egg white (optional)

- 2 to 3 dashes Bittermens 'Elemakule Tiki Bitters

1. Add all of the ingredients to a cocktail shaker and dry-shake before adding ice (if you're using egg white).

2. Continue to shake until the egg white is foamy and well incorporated. Add ice and shake until the drink is fully chilled.

3. Strain the cocktail over clean ice, preferably crushed, into a highball glass.

4. Garnish with freshly grated nutmeg.

BILLIE'S HOLIDAY

DEWEY'S JAZZ LOUNGE
232 WORTHINGTON STREET, SPRINGFIELD

Western Massachusetts often feels like a state separate from the eastern half dominated by Boston, with the Berkshire Mountains in one corner, and pleasant Connecticut River Valley towns hugging the shore from the Connecticut border up to Vermont and New Hampshire. By far the largest city in the area, Springfield is known for the museum that honors Theodor Geisel, aka children's author Dr. Seuss, who was born here. Thanks to educator James Naismith, the sport of basketball was invented here, and you can revel in all things hoops related at the Naismith Memorial Basketball Hall of Fame. This drink was created by co-owner Kenny Lumpkin, who honors the beloved chanteuse Billie Holiday with this elegant, beautiful drink that isn't afraid to pack a punch.

GLASSWARE: Champagne flute

GARNISH: Lemon wing

- 1½ oz. vodka
- ¾ oz. grenadine
- ½ oz. limoncello
- ½ oz. fresh lemon juice
- Champagne, to top

1. Add all of the ingredients, except the Champagne, to a mixing glass and stir.

2. Pour the mixture into a Champagne flute, then top with Champagne.

3. Garnish with a lemon wing.

PEAR MARTINI

BISTRO ZINC
56 CHURCH STREET, LENOX

Lenox is as far west as New Englanders can go in Massachusetts without hitting New York State, and yet they and 350,000 fellow music fans make the pilgrimage during the warm months to go to Tanglewood. This music center serves as the summer home of the Boston Symphony Orchestra and host to such legends as James Taylor, Joni Mitchell, Whitney Houston, and Bob Dylan. Even better, they can head into the town center for food and drink at refined but friendly places like Bistro Zinc, which offers French cuisine, original pieces by local artists on the walls, and luscious takes on classic libations. This Pear Martini, says general manager Max Dolan, is perfect for those hot summer days, and thus has been on the menu as long as he can remember.

GLASSWARE: Martini glass

- 3 oz. Grainger's Deluxe Organic Vodka
- 1 oz. pear liqueur
- Splash St. Elder Natural Elderflower Liqueur
- Splash freshly squeezed lime juice

1. Add all of the ingredients to a mixing glass and stir.
2. Pour the cocktail into a martini glass.

166 — NEW ENGLAND COCKTAILS

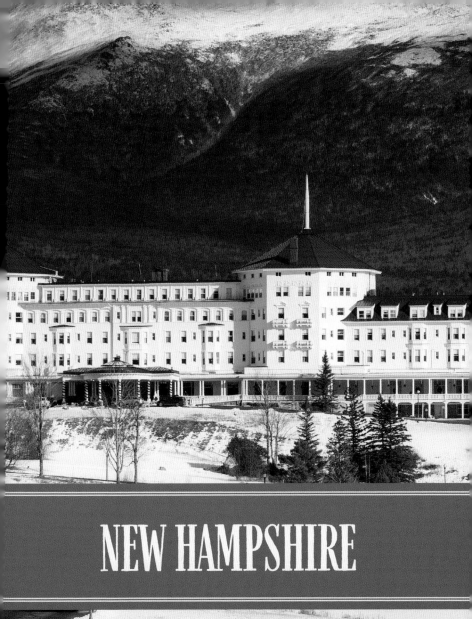

NEW HAMPSHIRE

UNCOMMON MANHATTAN

SIGNATURE MARGARITA

SPICED PALOMA

ORCHARD RITA

PRESIDENTIAL ESPRESSO MARTINI

COTTON'S SIGNATURE MANHATTAN

CHAI WHISKEY

SMOKE & A PANCAKE

PURPLE HAZE

LAVENDER GIN GIMLET

AQUABIT

New Hampshire often has the image of the tough, gritty New England state, with residents bearing the state's "Live Free or Die" motto on their car license plates. And historically, it's been the state that votes first in presidential primaries, where Democrat and Republican candidates first compete against each other for the support of voters who are proudly skeptical of boilerplate politicking. But that surface reputation barely does justice to this dramatically beautiful state, with lovely farms and towns galore, the very short but beachy Seacoast in the southeast, the extensive Lakes Region in the middle, and above all—literally and figuratively—the astonishing White Mountains up north. In fact, the Granite State can boast fifty-nine of the hundred highest mountains in the region, with Mount Washington being the tallest at 6,288 feet. All this makes New Hampshire a paradise for outdoor sports, especially skiing and hiking, and it also allows tourists an entry point to a land where the people may be feisty, but they're also friendly as hell too.

THE COMMON MAN

Any traveler driving north on Interstate 93 can't help but be welcomed along the way by various restaurants, convenience stores, inns, and delis up and down the state. The Common Man is a brand so ubiquitous along the tourist trail that its logo, featuring a ye olde farmer ploughing his field by hand, seems as common a state symbol as the Old Man of the Mountain. It's safe to say that The Common Man in whatever guise is often the first taste of hospitality that tourists get in the Granite State. Not bad for a local chain that began with just one restaurant in Ashland in 1971.

If The Common Man is often that interface between tourists and New Hampshire—in Lincoln, home of Loon Mountain, it is the après-ski spot par excellence—then Nicole White is the one who makes sure their drinks are up to snuff. Her title is officially "executive training manager," but overseeing the beverage department is a key part of the job. "We feel a big part of training our staff is not only how to produce the drinks, but also how to talk to the guests about what they're drinking," White says. "A lot of what we serve is made here in New England, often by small producers, meaning we bring in products that people don't always know. There's a fine line between what's hip and happening and that reflects our region and history, but also keeping to what people understand." As examples, she cites local vendors like Sap House Meadery in Ossipee and Tamworth Distilling (see page 316) in the town of the same name, which produces a ginger-root vodka for The Common Man. But she also makes sure the menu has simple twists on Manhattans, Margaritas, and Martinis. Either way, customers will learn that if they ask a question of their server or their bartender about a certain liquor, they can get an answer.

White herself knows intimately what it takes to create a good vibe in northern New England hospitality. She has worked in restaurants since she was a line cook in high school, and ten years ago, she joined

The Common Man in Ashland as a server, but only so she could pay off her college student loans. "It sounds very cliché," she laughs. "I fell in love with the company and its roots in the state. With so many locations, I could move my way from being a bartender to general manager, to my hybrid role of training and beverage."

This experience has come in handy when she's making up the cocktail menu that serves The Common Man restaurants—after all, it's probably the most widely consulted collection of drinks in the whole state, with half a million drinks poured across their locations each year. "I'm always trying to make something that will hit all points," White says. "Our locations are vastly different, yet similar. From a price point and from a trend standpoint, some locations bring in a lot of ski tourists, who are very different from our summer-lake-house tourists or our hikers that come through. Other locations are just popular with regulars in the town. Every demographic wants something different, so what works in one location doesn't in another. So you have to keep a balance, and you can never go wrong with the classics." The Common Man's most steady successes, in fact, have been the Uncommon Manhattan and Signature Margarita, each selling some 10,000 glasses every single year.

With New England comfort food, and a bar that often has a fireplace blazing, The Common Man, at any of its locations, is a cozy place to relax after whatever activity has been filling your day. And White is thrilled to make sure that the drink makes you feel at home too. "It's addictive to make people happy by giving them a cocktail that they love," she says. "It's a great business to be in. Most people are pretty happy when they're sitting down and having a cocktail."

OUTDOOR DINING
AVAILABLE
WWW.FLICKR.COM

UNCOMMON MANHATTAN

THE COMMON MAN

IO POLLARD ROAD, LINCOLN, AND OTHER LOCATIONS

Our Uncommon Manhattan has been a staple on our menu for at least ten to twelve years," says executive training manager Nicole White. "When people come in, they know what they're going to get already, and they're excited to have it again." And indeed, few drinks will warm you quite as well after a long day on the slopes.

—————————————— ❧ ——————————————

GLASSWARE: Martini glass, chilled

GARNISH: Luxardo cherry

- 2 oz. The Common Man Select Woodford Reserve Bourbon

- 1 oz. Carpano Antica Formula Vermouth

- 3 to 4 dashes cherry bitters

1. Add all of the ingredients to a cocktail shaker and stir.

2. Strain the cocktail into a chilled martini glass.

3. Garnish with a Luxardo cherry.

SIGNATURE MARGARITA

THE COMMON MAN
10 POLLARD ROAD, LINCOLN, AND OTHER LOCATIONS

The Common Man's other most popular cocktail, this Signature Margarita is perfect for New Hampshire's summer season of mountain biking, hiking, and boating. The sour mix that all the bartenders use is made and bottled by the restaurant company itself, and customers who favor its specific tart profile can buy a bottle of it too.

GLASSWARE: Margarita glass

GARNISH: Lime wedge

- 2 oz. Casa Noble Reposado Tequila
- ½ oz. Cointreau
- 2 oz. The Common Man Sour Mix

- ½ oz. fresh lime juice
- ½ oz. agave nectar
- Salt, for the rim
- ½ oz. Grand Marnier, to float

1. Combine all of the ingredients, except for the salt and Grand Marnier, over ice in a cocktail shaker.

2. Shake and pour the cocktail into a salt-rimmed margarita glass.

3. Float the Grand Marnier on top, and garnish with a lime wedge.

OMNI MOUNT WASHINGTON RESORT

310 MOUNT WASHINGTON HOTEL ROAD,
BRETTON WOODS

After winding along U.S. Route 302 for miles through the White Mountains National Forest, the trees open up and the view is breathtaking: a grand hotel, white with bright-red roofs, sprawling in a valley, set against the backdrop of Mount Washington and the Presidential Range. A four-season resort, it's a wonderland of alpine and Nordic skiing when the snow blankets everything, but when the snow is gone, you can try the eighteen-hole golf course, horseback riding, and hiking trails. The canopy tour can be done during any season and is not to be missed—it offers nine zip lines, two sky bridges, and three rappels as you soar as much as 165 feet above the forest floor. The hotel itself is dominated inside by a massive hearth in the Great Hall, and outside by its lengthy portico where guests can sit and admire the mountains. Naturally, it boasts many wonderful spaces to relax with a drink. And to jazz up your evening, head down to the basement and through a narrow door to The Cave, a Prohibition-style speakeasy lined with stone walls and customers partying the rest of the night away. Despite being surrounded and isolated by pristine forests and the highest summits in New England, you have all the social bustle you need right here.

SPICED PALOMA

ROSEBROOK BAR,
OMNI MOUNT WASHINGTON RESORT
310 MOUNT WASHINGTON HOTEL ROAD,
BRETTON WOODS

At the Rosebrook Bar, you can get small plates to eat and the Spiced Paloma, then enjoy it either out on the portico or at a table inside—they both have the same majestic view. An even more expansive panorama greets you at the Switchback Grille at the Rosebrook Lodge, atop the Bretton Woods Ski Area: there you can marvel at the mountains and the hotel far below as you sip an après-ski drink to warm you up.

※

GLASSWARE: Rocks glass

GARNISH: Lime slice

- 1½ oz. Casamigos Blanco Tequila
- 1½ oz. grapefruit juice
- 1 oz. cinnamon simple syrup
- ¼ oz. lime juice

1. Combine all of the ingredients in a cocktail shaker and shake well.

2. Pour the cocktail over ice into a rocks glass.

3. Garnish with a lime slice.

ORCHARD RITA

The Omni's elegant main dining room dates back to 1902, and it is the showpiece of the resort's various restaurant experiences. In the morning, you can get a sumptuous brunch as the sun streams in over the White Mountains, and then at night, it's transformed into an elegant, chandelier-lit venue offering clams casino, beef tournedos, and Moroccan tagine, among many other culinary specialties. And if you want an eclectic drink, like this Orchard Rita, you can get it at your dinner table or at the hightop bar in the center of the dining room.

GLASSWARE: Collins glass

GARNISH: Green apple slice

- 2 oz. freshly squeezed apple juice
- 1¼ oz. Casamigos Añejo Tequila
- 1 oz. fresh-pressed cucumber juice
- ¼ oz. lime juice
- Maple-lime salt, for the rim

1. Combine all of the ingredients in a cocktail shaker and shake well.

2. Pour the cocktail over ice into a collins glass with a maple-lime salt rim.

PRESIDENTIAL ESPRESSO MARTINI

STICKNEY'S STEAK & CHOP PUB,
OMNI MOUNT WASHINGTON RESORT
310 MOUNT WASHINGTON HOTEL ROAD,
BRETTON WOODS

At the more casual Stickney's Restaurant, this take on an Espresso Martini offers a decadent dessert to follow up on that 16 oz. dry-aged New York strip steak, 12 oz. Kurobuta pork chop, or seared scallops with black garlic risotto.

— ✤ —

GLASSWARE: Martini glass

GARNISH: Chocolate espresso beans (optional)

- 1½ oz. chilled espresso
- 1¼ oz. Tito's Handmade Vodka
- ¾ oz. Kahlúa
- ½ oz. Tempus Fugit Crème de Cacao
- ¼ oz. Liber & Co Demerara Syrup

1. Combine all of the ingredients in a cocktail shaker and shake well.

2. Pour the cocktail over ice into a martini glass.

3. Garnish with chocolate espresso beans, if you like.

COTTON

Manchester is by far New Hampshire's largest city, albeit with a population of just about 115,000 people, but it's best known for being one of the largest industrial centers in early American history. Settled in the early 1700s on the shores of the Merrimack River, it was originally known by more bucolic names like its Pennacook name Amoskeag ("good fishing place"), Nutfield, and Derryfield, until a manufacturer named Samuel Blodget claimed in the early 1800s that the burgeoning burg would become "the Manchester of America," after the English city then leading the Industrial Revolution. So in 1810, the city gained its new name and set about building a manufacturing metropolis that still boggles the eye and mind, with its mile-and-a-half-long stretch of brick colossi called the Millyard still towering over the riverbank. The development was spearheaded by the Amoskeag Manufacturing Company, and by 1910, it was the largest textile company in the world, with 17,000 workers producing a total of five million yards of cloth each day. Soon enough, though, increasingly obsolete technology and labor strife took their toll, as was the case in so many New England mill cities, and Amoskeag Manufacturing went bankrupt in 1935. The once-thriving Manchester went into decades of decline.

The good news these days is that the city has gone through quite a revitalization, with the Millyard and the riverfront bursting with new companies and nightlife. One of the key pioneers of this renaissance for the Queen City is a restaurant owned by Jeffrey and Peaches Paige, appropriately called Cotton. It opened in the Millyard in 2000, sited in an old Amoskeag Manufacturing outbuilding that once served as the blacksmith shop. Cotton has been one of those restaurants that every city needs to boost a dining scene, with a strong emphasis on fine dining and fine cocktails but made accessible in a casual setting. Regularly cited as one of the best restaurants in the state by publications ranging from the regional *Yankee* magazine to *Bon Appétit*, it's still going strong, thanks to the talent and verve of this husband-and-wife duo.

When you talk to Peaches Paige, you immediately are taken in by her enthusiasm. For example, she's an avid student of the up-and-down history of Cotton's location, whether it's the achievements of the massive factories or the fact that the country's first breakout of anthrax happened here in 1957, thanks to infected goat hair in a mill that is now her parking lot. "Every timber and brick went through an incinerator and got buried down in Singer Family Park," she notes with fascination.

But she's particularly excited to talk about cocktails. Jeffrey is the chef in the kitchen, while the bar is her domain, where cocktails are the main draw. "You think people would order wine," she says, "but I sell way more booze than wine. All my liquor reps show me everything and leave me samples, so I go behind the bar when nobody's here and play around. Then I bring it to Jeff to try it out." She always creates her cocktails the fundamental way, by focusing on a base spirit like whiskey or gin, then adding something new to bring the flavor profile out. Take her Chai Whisky, for example, which combines Suntory Whisky from Japan with the complex liqueurs Falernum and Licor 43, then adds a masala chai tea bag that continues to steep as you sip.

One ingredient she uses often, especially in Cotton's Signature Manhattan, is the bourbon custom-made for them by Woodford Reserve. Back in 2015, the restaurant was the top seller of Woodford Reserve in New Hampshire, so the Paiges were invited to Kentucky to create their own whiskey. Jeff and Paige sampled various barrels with one of the distillers and compared tasting notes. They chose two separate barrels that complemented each other, which were then combined to make their own blend. Each barrel they've ordered yields the equivalent of 188 bottles of bourbon, Peaches says, and they're still rolling them in.

But despite all this experimenting and custom distilling, Peaches is also aware that the people who work for her have to sling a lot of drinks quickly to a busy room of diners. In the end, her approach sums up the blunt pragmatism so emblematic of her city and her state. "My philosophy is to keep it simple; use really good ingredients," she says. "I don't want to make anything too complicated because my bartenders will kill me. After all, they are the ones who have to make it."

COTTON'S SIGNATURE MANHATTAN

COTTON

75 ARMS STREET, MANCHESTER

Sure, not everyone can just jaunt off to Kentucky and make their own blend of bourbon, but if you buy your own bottle of Woodford Reserve bourbon and its accompanying spiced cherry bitters, you can get pretty close to Cotton's sublime take on this classic.

— ❧ —

GLASSWARE: Martini glass, chilled
GARNISH: Luxardo cherry

- 2½ oz. Cotton Select Woodford Reserve Bourbon
- ½ oz. Carpano Antica Formula Vermouth
- 3 dashes Woodford Reserve Spiced Cherry Bitters

1. Add ice to a Boston shaker until half-full, then add all of the ingredients.

2. Stir about ten times with a barspoon.

3. Strain the contents into a chilled martini glass and garnish with a Luxardo cherry.

CHAI WHISKEY

J ust for that très Cottonesque blend of sleek sophistication and creative whimsy, Peaches Paige offers this cozy cocktail that functions as both your evening tea and your evening tipple.

〜

GLASSWARE: Martini glass, chilled
GARNISH: Luxardo cherry

- 1 Mighty Leaf Masala Chai Tea Bag
- 2 oz. Suntory Whisky
- ½ oz. The Bitter Truth Golden Falernum
- ½ oz. Licor 43

1. Put the Mighty Leaf Masala Chai Tea bag in a metal container and add 2 oz. boiling water. Allow the tea to steep while preparing the cocktail.

2. Fill a Boston shaker with ice and add the whiskey, Falernum, and Licor 43.

3. Add the 2 oz. of steeped tea to the shaker—do not add the tea bag. Put on the cover of the shaker and shake vigorously.

4. Strain the cocktail into a chilled martini glass.

5. Garnish with a Luxardo cherry and the silk-lined tea bag that was already being steeped for this drink. The tea bag will continue to steep and add more flavor as you sip the cocktail.

SMOKE & A PANCAKE

815 COCKTAILS & PROVISIONS
815 ELM STREET, MANCHESTER

Elm Street is the main drag through the city of Manchester, and at three and a half miles long, it has the odd reputation of being the longest double dead-end street in the country. But despite petering out into cul-de-sacs at either end, in the middle, it's a wide, bustling thoroughfare that in recent years has become lined with eclectic places to go out to. At 815, you will find one of its most friendly bars to imbibe, with a vintage vibe highlighted by comfy couches, mismatched chairs, dark lace curtains, and a brick wall bearing the slogan in big block lettering: "VOTE AGAINST PROHIBITION." It's also a place where owners Ryan McCabe and Sarah Maillet can offer you a choice selection of craft beers and rare whiskeys, as well as this smoky yet tropical take on an Old Fashioned.

GLASSWARE: Rocks glass

GARNISH: Pineapple slice

- 2 oz. Charred Pineapple–Infused Del Maguey Vida Mezcal (see recipe)
- ½ oz. demerara sugar
- 3 dashes chicory bitters
- Expressed orange peel
- Luxardo cherry

1. Combine all of the ingredients in a mixing glass and stir.

2. Pour the cocktail into a rocks glass over a 2-inch ice cube.

3. Garnish with a pineapple slice.

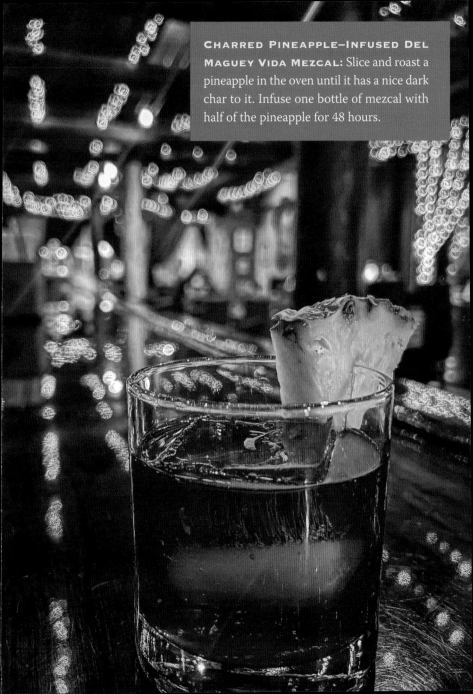

CHARRED PINEAPPLE–INFUSED DEL MAGUEY VIDA MEZCAL: Slice and roast a pineapple in the oven until it has a nice dark char to it. Infuse one bottle of mezcal with half of the pineapple for 48 hours.

PURPLE HAZE

Just one block off busy Elm Street lies an inviting bistro that can serve as a place to start your evening, or as a place to spend a whole night out. Opened in 2008 by the brother-sister team of chef David Becker and manager Diane Downing, it fills the first floor of an old brick building with warm light and the scents of a menu that melds Italian, Asian, New Orleans, and New England seafood dishes. And Firefly's cocktails offer deliciously intriguing mash-ups, like the Purple Haze here, a citrus concoction that gets its alluring color from the indigo gin tinged with butterfly pea flowers.

GLASSWARE: Highball glass

GARNISH: 2 gooseberries or a lemon wedge

- ½ oz. Meyer lemon juice
- 3 oz. tangerine juice
- 1 oz. elderflower liqueur
- 2½ oz. Empress 1908 Indigo Gin

1. Combine all of the ingredients, except the gin, in a shaker filled with ice.

2. Shake thoroughly.

3. Strain the cocktail over ice into a highball glass.

4. Slowly pour the gin over the mixture so that it floats on top.

5. Garnish with the gooseberries, or with a lemon wedge if gooseberries aren't in season.

LAVENDER GIN GIMLET

FIREFLY BISTRO & BAR

22 CONCORD STREET, MANCHESTER

The Lavender Gin Gimlet adds the flavor of Provence's iconic flower to this classic British cocktail. Whether you wish to make it even fancier and heartier with an egg white is up to you, but it is recommended.

⊗

GLASSWARE: Coupe glass

GARNISH: Lime slice

- 4 oz. The Botanist Islay Dry Gin
- 1 oz. key lime juice
- 1 oz. lavender simple syrup
- ½ oz. agave nectar

1. Combine all of the ingredients in a shaker with ice.

2. Shake vigorously.

3. Strain into a coupe and garnish with a lime slice.

AQUABIT

BOTANICA RESTAURANT AND GIN BAR
110 BREWERY LANE, SUITE 105, PORTSMOUTH

Less than twenty miles along the Atlantic Ocean, New Hampshire's coastline is the shortest of any coastal American state, but the Seacoast region makes up for its small size by packing itself with fun destinations. Not only are seaside towns like Hampton Beach hopping with people in the summer, but the city of Portsmouth is a happening city all year long. It boasts some creative bars and restaurants, like Botanica, which stays true to its name by pairing its French cuisine with that most botanical of base spirits: gin. With limited space for his bar, owner and chef Brendan Vesey decided to focus on gin, stocking a deep selection that reflects the vast array of flavor profiles that it can have. After that, there is no limit to its creative uses, like this frothy magenta gem that gains extra herbaceous punch from the aquavit and toasted caraway seeds. To prepare this as a great mocktail, replace the alcohol with caraway syrup and double the amount of shrub.

— ಬಿ —

GLASSWARE: Collins glass
GARNISH: Candied Caraway Seeds (see recipe)

- 1½ oz. Beet Shrub (see recipe)
- 1 oz. Tamworth Distilling Skiklubben Aquavit
- 1 oz. gin
- 1 oz. egg white or aquafaba
- ½ oz. lemon juice
- Soda water, to top

1. Add all of the ingredients, except the soda water, to a mixing glass.

2. Dry-shake vigorously to develop a foam.

3. Add ice (large cubes make better foam) and shake again.

4. Strain the cocktail into a collins glass, and gently pour soda water down a barspoon to lift the foam to the top of the glass . . . and over the top, if you are feeling adventurous.

5. Garnish with the Candied Caraway Seeds.

BEET SHRUB: Wash and chop one large beet, then add to a jar and cover with apple cider vinegar for 3 to 5 days. Purée and strain the mixture and reserve the liquid. Then toast 1 tbsp. caraway seeds and 1 tsp. black pepper in a small saucepan. Once the mixture is fragrant, add 1 cup water and 1 cup sugar, and bring to a boil. Simmer for 10 minutes, then strain it into the beet-and-vinegar mixture that had been set aside.

CANDIED CARAWAY SEEDS: Toast ½ cup caraway seeds in a small skillet until fragrant, then toss in powdered sugar while warm, with a few drops of water. Shake in a basket strainer to remove excess sugar. Lay the seeds out to dry on a paper towel or dehydrate them.

RHODE ISLAND

JUJU JUICE

FEELING WAVY

MANGO CAIPIRINHA

ZUCCHINI | HERBES DE PROVENCE

WATERMELON | RHUBARB

HOT CLUB MARGARITA

THE PORT OLD FASHIONED

SMOKED OLD FASHIONED

NORTHERN LIGHTS

BLACK MAGIC SANGRIA

ROSYAY!

PURPLE MARTIN

Ah yes, Little Rhody . . . it's the affectionate nickname for what is by far the smallest state in the United States by land area. Hemmed in by Connecticut and Massachusetts, one can pass through it in the blink of an eye. But then you'd be missing some of the loveliest towns and coastlines in the country. Indeed, this state is dominated by open water, whether it's the endless beaches on the southwest coast and the shores of Narragansett Bay, or the high-profile, high-income island town of Newport, which explodes as one of New England's party headquarters in the summer. And, of course, there's culturally rich Providence, one of the region's largest cities, home to vanguard colleges like Brown University, Rhode Island School of Design, and the renowned culinary arts program at Johnson & Wales University. Spend some time in Little Rhody, and it starts to seem quite large indeed.

KIN SOUTHERN TABLE + BAR

71 WASHINGTON STREET, PROVIDENCE

A conversation with Julia Broome is like getting a hearty hug. Quick with a buoyant laugh that reflects a charming air of positivity, this restaurateur brings the same bonhomie to her downtown Providence spot, Kin Southern Table + Bar, and that's all by design. "It really starts at the door," she says. "When anyone comes in, our goal is to attack them with love. One of the first pieces of artwork you'll see says, 'If the love doesn't feel like 1990s R & B, I don't want it.'" Of course, once you're in the door, Kin pairs sweet grooves on the stereo with Dixie delights like fried green tomatoes, chicken and waffles, and barbecue pulled-pork sliders. And then there are the "dranks," which add a bright, fruity vibe to the night. "When you think 'classic cocktails,' you think of Old Fashioneds and very strong dude drinks," Broome says with a laugh. "But we wanted to make our cocktails fun and interactive and pretty, and sometimes girly. We just want people to have these fun cocktails, then go out and explore the city."

Broome herself was born and raised in Providence, with family roots going back to Upstate New York and Virginia. Growing up, she says, her parents always had a few places to go to connect with the community and bring people together, and soon she was "hospitality all the way," getting her first job working at a Chuck E. Cheese. After getting a degree in marketing at Boston University, she worked for the Greater Boston Convention & Visitors Bureau, then as an event manager and trade-show representative. Then the COVID pandemic hit in 2020, and at 33 years old, she was laid off. But Broome put her tireless optimism and work ethic to use: "I figured I'd do something productive and take advantage of this time to myself. I figured I'd put together what my ideal restaurant would look and feel like, but then soon enough I was signing a lease, and all these plans became super real."

During that period, the pandemic also separated Broome from her usual social calendar, making her miss times with family, summer barbecues, the good food, and a sense of community coming together, so that's where her idea of an extrovertedly welcoming spot came into play. The concept for her drink menu also came from time spent with friends. "The first thing that came to mind was definitely rum," she says. "During the fun times I've had experimenting with beverages, I had been making some fun punches. Even going back to my senior year at BU, we always had a fun rum punch, which evolved into the Juju Juice we have today. Other drinks came from other trips I've had: Auntie's Kool-Aid is based on a drink I had in Detroit, while One Night in Miami is literally a drink I had in Miami. It speaks to my travel experiences and doing cool things with other people."

She also chose rum as the fundamental basis of her cocktail menu to celebrate the African diaspora, since, after all, so much rum is made in the sugarcane islands of the Caribbean, and its history dates back to the slavery days of the Triangle Trade. Despite whiskey being so often associated with Southern food, she felt rum was underappreciated, and aimed to get drinkers to diversify their palates, so her bar highlights rums from locales like St. Lucia and Trinidad, Brazilian cachaça, local spirits from Rhode Island and Boston, and even rapper Lil Wayne's Bumbu Rum ("Eh, why not?" she avers). Meanwhile, the stereo is always playing a warm mix of Black artists from throughout the ages, from doo-wop to R & B to Afrobeat and hip-hop, as well as her parents' beloved Earth, Wind & Fire and Stevie Wonder.

The event planner in her has also inspired ways for Kin Southern Table to broaden its embrace of the wider community. The restaurant has hosted a Mardi Gras party, where a local drum troupe came through and performed while patrons downed beignets and po' boys with their drinks. She has started a series of mixers to get singles to meet each other—always careful to keep a healthy male-female attendance ratio—and every Juneteenth since she opened, she's hosted a block party downtown to celebrate this vital holiday in Black history. And it's also another excuse to get everyone to converge downtown for funky music and killer food, because that's her goal: to bring not just customers together, but the whole city.

"Growing up on the south side, it was easy to stay in your little neighborhood and only venture downtown when something big was happening," Broome says. "With this place, I knew I wanted it to be centralized, so that no matter what neighborhood you live in, you could drive here easily or catch the bus down here, feel comfortable, get people to step out of their shells and have some fun."

JUJU JUICE

KIN SOUTHERN TABLE + BAR
71 WASHINGTON STREET, PROVIDENCE

Inspired by the fruity concoctions she came up with in college, owner Julia Broome has perfected the libation to get any party with friends started, whether you're celebrating at Kin Southern Table or at home.

&

GLASSWARE: Tiki mug

GARNISH: Lime slice

- 1½ oz. pineapple juice
- 1½ oz. mango juice
- 1 oz. Bacardí Black Rum
- 1 oz. Bacardi Coconut Rum
- Splash lime juice
- Splash grenadine

1. Combine all of the ingredients in a shaker full of ice.

2. Shake! Shake! Shake!

3. Pour the drink into a tiki mug over ice.

4. Garnish with a lime slice..

FEELING WAVY

KIN SOUTHERN TABLE + BAR

71 WASHINGTON STREET, PROVIDENCE

A great tiki drink needs to send you drifitng off to the sun-soaked beach in your mind, and this bright blend excels at that task, with its tropical flavors and overproof rum distilled just down the shore in the resort town of Newport.

❧

GLASSWARE: Tiki mug

GARNISH: Cherry, orange slice

- 2 oz. pineapple juice
- 1½ oz. Thomas Tew Widows Walk Rum
- ¾ oz. blue curaçao
- ¾ oz. cream of coconut
- ½ oz. lemonade

1. Combine all of the ingredients in a shaker full of ice.

2. Shake.

3. Pour the cocktail into a tiki mug over ice.

4. Garnish with a cherry and an orange slice.

MANGO CAIPIRINHA

THE DEAN BAR
122 FOUNTAIN STREET, PROVIDENCE

The Dean is downtown Providence's hippest boutique hotel, perhaps made even more decadently hip by the fact that this four-story brick building was built in 1911 as a brothel. But aside from its cool image and sleek rooms, The Dean has preserved many of the old features, such as the original mosaic tile floor and the cage elevator. It also houses The Dean Bar, an evocative, dimly lit craft cocktail bar, perfect for those chillaxing moments or a romantic tryst.

Michael Silva is the restaurant and bar manager at the hotel, and he offers here his most popular cocktail on the menu, a glass full of flavor. "This cocktail is very special to me because of the spirit we use for our base," Silva says. "It's called 'grogue,' which is basically a West African cachaça that comes from Cape Verde, and the flavor profile reminds me of a family breakfast we would have at a restaurant where I used to work."

GLASSWARE: Tall tiki glass

GARNISH: Cilantro leaf

- 1 cilantro leaf
- Pinch kosher salt
- 1 oz. mango syrup

- 1½ oz. Tropicana Grog Extra
- ½ oz. Pelotón de la Muerte Mezcal Artesanal
- 1 oz. lime juice

1. Start by adding the cilantro leaf and salt into a shaker.

2. Add the remaining ingredients, starting with the mango syrup.

3. Shake vigorously with one ice cube.

4. Pour the cocktail into a tall tiki glass filled with crushed ice.

5. Garnish with a cilantro leaf.

MARCELINO'S BOUTIQUE BAR

The Omni Providence Hotel towers above the city with glorious views of the state capitol building in one direction; in the other direction, guests can see the Providence River widen out into Narragansett Bay. But on the ground, the doors on the windswept corner of Exchange and Fountain streets lead you into an otherworldly experience at Marcelino's Boutique Bar. With an ideal balance of opulent lights, evocative shadows, and atmospheric music, the space feels larger than it is as you choose whether to sit at the bar, a low-top table, or even in an intimate speakeasy room. And then there are the cocktails. Simply named after pairs of flavors—like "Pineapple/Vetiver"—these carefully handcrafted drinks themselves are each an intriguing bounty, delicious but complex, presented with naturalistic garnishes clipped to the side of the glass. It's a getaway where you will want to spend hours, and it's a vision whose origins lie thousands of miles away in the Middle East.

Marcelino Abou Ali grew up in Batroun, Lebanon, a seaside city that is one of the oldest inhabited municipalities in the world. His grandparents were farmers, growing oranges, peaches, tomatoes, and any number of vegetables, and being around them inspires him to this day. "When my grandmother wanted to make tomato paste, I could always smell her smoking the tomatoes. We grew up like other people there, creating and crafting everything, since back then you had to have a field in order to eat. Whatever you need, you just have to make yourself."

By the time he was a teenager, Marcelino was sleeping on the first floor of his grandmother's house so he could sneak out at night and work in the clubs in the resort town of Jounieh, a half hour's drive down the coast. In 2007, at a beach bar there, Marcelino's manager introduced him to another young nightlife upstart named Refaat Ghostine, and their friendship and careers have been linked together since then. Over the next few years, the two young men worked their way up from being barbacks in Jounieh to working in Beirut's premier club, Buddha Bar. Marcelino eventually would travel around the region doing star turns working as a "flair bartender," delivering drinks with dazzling feats of bottle-tossing acrobatics, and investing in new bars and clubs as a partner. Meanwhile, in 2014, Refaat became head bartender at Beirut's Central Station Boutique Bar, where he gained renown for his creative use of a rotary evaporator for vacuum distilling and centrifuge for separating and clarifying ingredients. Central Station was a regular on the World's 50 Best Bars annual list, and Refaat himself was named World Class Country Winner by Diageo in 2015.

Nevertheless, the United States beckoned when Marcelino's family moved to New England in 2015 so that his younger brother, Pascal, could go to school there, and Marcelino found himself in Rhode Island starting his career over again, working tirelessly anywhere he could, whether at a gas station or finally managing a place in Federal Hill, Providence's Little Italy. And it was there that he made his name with customers for his professional service as a host, and where his dream of opening his own place came to fruition, thanks to one of his regulars, a dentist named Basel Badawi. "I gave him very good service; he liked my attitude and discipline and asked me what's my goal," Marcelino says. "I said I'm working toward it; I want to open an experience, I want to build a brand. But to start, I need a space. And he said, 'Why don't we do this thing together?'" And so the two men became partners, and then in 2018, when they signed for the space on the ground floor of the Omni, they became co-owners of Marcelino's Boutique Bar.

Marcelino immediately obsessed about the challenging, warren-like space, carefully choosing every lighting fixture, every decoration in every nook, every music speaker in every room. With his experience, he knew he could do a good job with creating a cocktail program, but he felt that if he did his best with the interior design, why not get the best bartender he knows? Refaat was working in Dubai at the time, and when Marcelino asked him to come to his adopted home state to create a bar, Refaat asked what island he was talking about. "I said, 'Rhode Island,'" Marcelino laughs. "He thought it was actually an island! But then he came here and inspired people. He's the cream on top of the cake."

The bar opened in 2020, with the cocktail menu created by Refaat, using the fundamental flavors and ingredients of the Middle East that they grew up eating and drinking, and applying the advanced techniques that he perfected back home. And it was also Refaat's idea to keep the cocktail names bluntly simple, both to do something different, but also to give customers a clear idea of what their drink will taste like. "I do believe in getting straight to the point," Marcelino says. "Not everybody is a bartender, so you can't expect people to just understand what you're tasting. So we made it in a way to get to people's minds and hearts with the title, so they can understand more and help them make a better choice."

Now with his old friend bringing his artistry to his adopted hometown, and even with his brother, Pascal, doing the accounting and purchasing, Marcelino has seen his aspirations come full circle. "Even when I was a kid in school, I dreamed about coming to America, even if I didn't know much about it," he says. "And now this place feels like home. It was a long way from 2015 to opening in 2020, but if it wasn't challenging, it would have been boring."

Beverage director Refaat Ghostine says that he created this cocktail as a tribute to the region defined by the legendary sea that washes up on his home country's shores: "The use of zucchini is a nod to Lebanese cuisine, while the herbes de Provence blend reflects the Mediterranean influence." The result is a refreshing drink with a healthy vegetal vibe that gains complexity from the dry sherry, and he says shaking is crucial for getting that irresistible frothy texture.

— ☙ —

GLASSWARE: Collins glass

GARNISH: Zucchini jerky

- **40 ml olive oil fat-washed vodka & gin blend**
- **30 ml zucchini puree**
- **20 ml lemon juice**
- **10 ml herbes de Provence–infused Cocchi Americano**
- **10 ml dry sherry**

1. Add all of the ingredients to a shaker filled with ice.

2. Shake well.

3. Fine-strain the cocktail over ice into a collins glass.

4. Garnish with a piece of zucchini jerky.

WATERMELON | RHUBARB

MARCELINO'S BOUTIQUE BAR
I WEST EXCHANGE STREET, PROVIDENCE

If this bright cocktail from Marcelino's bar director, Refaat Ghostine, makes you want to sit out-side and take in (or dream of) warm breezes, that's no accident. "Drawing from the flavors that graced my youthful palate," bar director Refaat Ghostine says, "the cocktail begins its journey with a base of rhubarb-infused gin, with a delicate tang in every sip. Aperol dances in, adding a slightly orange bitter note, reminiscent of the sunsets that colored my Lebanese evenings. But it's the house-made watermelon cordial that captures the heart of the season— refreshing, sweet, and reminiscent of the lazy afternoons I spent devouring watermelon slices. With a burst of lemon juice, the cocktail takes on a zesty vitality, mirroring the laughter that echoed through those carefree days. As the layers unfold, a surprise emerges—a feta cheese foam that crowns the elixir, elevating it into a realm of savory indulgence. This creamy crown is an ode to the pairing of watermelon and feta cheese, emblematic of my childhood snacking delight."

GLASSWARE: Old-fashioned glass
GARNISH: Dried oregano

- 50 ml rhubarb-infused gin
- 30 ml watermelon cordial
- 20 ml lemon juice
- 10 ml Aperol
- Feta cheese foam, to top

1. Add all of the ingredients, except for the feta cheese foam, to a shaker filled with ice.

2. Shake well, then fine-strain the cocktail over one big cube of ice into an old-fashioned glass.

3. Top with the feta cheese foam, and garnish with dried oregano.

HOT CLUB
25 BRIDGE STREET, PROVIDENCE

Located right where the Providence River widens out into the harbor, the Hot Club has long been the city's go-to place for a relaxed waterfront gathering. Its huge neon sign has been an iconic fixture in the city for decades. Back in 1981, friends Josh Miller and Tom Bates bought a tiny abandoned brick building on a dirt road by the river, envisioning such a social hub, but most people thought they were crazy. Back then, Providence was not the modern cultural hot spot it is today, but a postindustrial northeastern city with a decaying urban core and neglected waterfront. Miller and Bates started with a humble twelve seater, and they named it after both a Parisian nightclub and the building's former life as the boiler room for the steam engine factory across the street. The Hot Club soon became the place to be, and you're always guaranteed a fun night out with a fruity cocktail in hand, including their house Margarita.

ॐ

GLASSWARE: Margarita glass
GARNISH: Lime wedge

- Salt, for the rim (optional)
- 2 oz. tequila
- 1 oz. sour mix
- ½ oz. triple sec

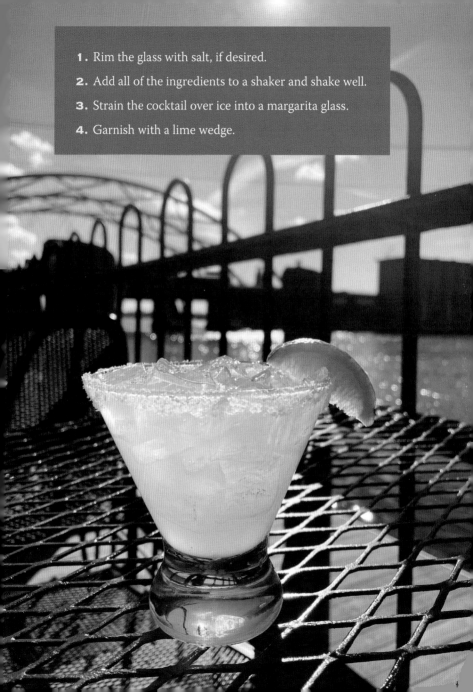

1. Rim the glass with salt, if desired.
2. Add all of the ingredients to a shaker and shake well.
3. Strain the cocktail over ice into a margarita glass.
4. Garnish with a lime wedge.

THE PORT OLD FASHIONED

FORTY 1° NORTH

351 THAMES STREET, NEWPORT

Newport is a small city hanging on the southernmost end of Aquidneck Island, where Narragansett Bay meets the Atlantic Ocean. Its supreme location means that it has had a long maritime history. But let's face it, Newport is really known for being a seaside resort for the überwealthy and a party town for the rest of us. You can go to the beach, or bike around the coast, or stroll the Cliff Walk and check out all the colossal Gilded Age mansions on the island. In the summer, be sure to head to the Pavilion Bar section of the complex, which sits on the water overlooking the superyachts in the marina. With that view and this drink in your hand, you'll feel like a dynastic tycoon yourself.

GLASSWARE: Rocks glass

GARNISH: Orange peel, expressed; Luxardo cherry

- 1 oz. bourbon
- 1 oz. rye whiskey
- Angostura bitters, to taste
- ¼ oz. Port Wine Demerara (see recipe)

1. Blend the bourbon and rye together in a container of your choice.
2. Start with a few dashes of the bitters in a stir tin.
3. Add the blended whiskey and the Port Wine Demerara.
4. Add ice and stir for 15 to 20 seconds, or until the ice begins to melt.
5. Strain the cocktail over fresh ice in a rocks glass.
6. Garnish with an expressed orange peel and a Luxardo cherry.

PORT WINE DEMERARA: Combine two parts port wine and one part demerara sugar, then heat the mixture, stirring until the sugar has dissolved.

SMOKED OLD FASHIONED

WHITE HORSE TAVERN
26 MARLBOROUGH STREET, NEWPORT

Having opened in 1673, the White Horse Tavern is a National Historic Landmark—after all, it's the oldest operating restaurant in the United States, and is regularly cited as one of the ten oldest in the world. And it's hard not to notice the Colonial architecture of its crimson façade, nor is it hard to feel welcome in its cozy interior, where the general assembly used to meet when Rhode Island was still a colony. A few years ago, general manager Jarred LaPlante was working with one of his bartenders to update the fall cocktail menu, playing around with smoked bourbon that they make in-house with apple chips. Once they added the vanilla syrup behind the bar and some black walnut bitters found stashed in the back room, they had a drink that's been on the menu ever since, regardless of the season.

GLASSWARE: Rocks glass
GARNISH: Amarena cherry, orange peel

- 1 Amarena cherry
- 1 orange peel
- ½ oz. vanilla syrup

- 4 to 5 dashes black walnut bitters
- 2 oz. Wood-Smoked Four Roses Bourbon (see recipe)

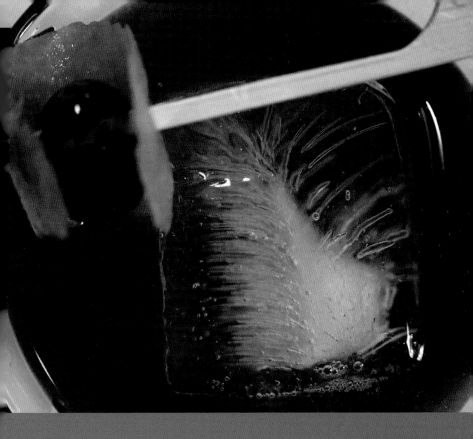

1. In a rocks glass, muddle the cherry and orange peel with the vanilla syrup and black walnut bitters.

2. Add the smoked bourbon and ice.

3. Garnish with another cherry and orange peel.

WOOD-SMOKED FOUR ROSES BOURBON: Take a quart of wood chips—the White Horse Tavern uses apple wood—and soak them in water for 20 to 30 minutes. Strain the wood chips and place them in a single layer. Torch the wood chips until they start to smoke, then place them in a jar. Pour the bourbon over the wood chips, let the infusion sit for 3 days, then strain.

NORTHERN LIGHTS

COAST GUARD HOUSE

40 OCEAN ROAD, NARRAGANSETT

Rhode Island has fabulous beaches on its southwest coast, and the eastern side of Narragansett Bay has old scenic harbor towns. But in the end, it's the west side of the bay that boasts the state's best beach town, itself called Narragansett. Where Newport has the mansions and the moneyed glitterati to go with them, Narragansett is more low-key and relaxed, with ice cream stands, surf shops, and seafood joints. It also has The Coast Guard House, a historic restaurant first built in the 1940s that has been popular ever since, thanks in part to stunning waterfront views. The setting is so lovely that in 2023, OpenTable named Coast Guard House one of the most romantic restaurants in America. And now thanks to cocktail director Fred Koury, you can toast your special someone with this drink.

GLASSWARE: Large wineglass

GARNISH: Lemon twist

- 1½ oz. Empress 1908 Gin
- ½ oz. St. Elder Natural Elderflower Liqueur
- Lemon juice, to taste
- Orange bitters, to taste
- Prosecco, to top

1. Pour the gin and the St. Elder into a large wineglass.

2. Add lemon juice and a few drops of orange bitters, then fill the glass with ice.

3. Top with prosecco, and garnish with a lemon twist.

BLACK MAGIC SANGRIA

COAST GUARD HOUSE

40 OCEAN ROAD, NARRAGANSETT

S angria might as well be one of the official drinks of a hot American summer, perfect for the extensive views of Narragansett surf. But of course, New Englanders are always aware that autumn is just around the corner, and with its cinnamon and apple cider, this sangria certainly will carry you through leaf-peeping season.

❧

GLASSWARE: Large wineglass

GARNISH: Cinnamon stick, cherries, orange slice

- 1½ oz. Captain Morgan Original Spiced Rum
- 1 oz. apple cider
- 1 oz. blood orange cranberry juice
- 1 teaspoon passion fruit puree
- Pinot noir, to top

1. In a shaker, add ice, then the remaining ingredients, except the wine.

2. Shake well.

3. Pour the mixture into a large wineglass and top with pinot noir.

4. Garnish with a cinnamon stick, cherries, and an orange slice.

OCEAN HOUSE

1 BLUFF AVENUE, WATCH HILL

Watch Hill is as far west as you can go along the Rhode Island coast before you hit Connecticut. In fact, most of the land you see across the water is the Constitution State waving hello. But in this distant outpost, you can find one of New England's poshest resort villages, home of the Holiday House, where libertine oil heiress Rebekah West Harkness once lived and filled the pool with bubbly for extravagant parties—it's now owned by pop superstar Taylor Swift, who retold the whole story in her song "The Last Great American Dynasty." But just down the street from Holiday House is a complex even more grand.

The Ocean House is a huge, champagne-colored resort spread on a bluff, adorned with broad, curvaceous wraparound porches and even a croquet lawn on the side. Surrounded by greenery, a walkway descends to a beach lined with cabanas. You could spend all day lounging here, or you could shop on Bay Street, walk over to the Watch Hill Lighthouse, or hike around the sand dunes and old forts of Napatree Point Conservation Area. Whatever you do, you'll spend your evenings having a drink at the hotel or at its sister property a couple of beaches down the road. And when you get home, you'll make this offering from Jonathan Feiler, Ocean House's wine and beverage director, to remind you of when you hobnobbed with ghosts of gentry past and present.

ROSYAY!

S o, how do you finish a day of swimming, beaching, hiking, and shopping—perhaps with a round of croquet slotted into your gloriously full vacation schedule? Well, you kick back at the Ocean House with this light, rosy, refreshing breeze of a cocktail.

જી

GLASSWARE: White wineglass

GARNISH: Cherries or orange slice

- 3 oz. rosé
- 1½ oz. vodka

- Splash pomegranate juice, grenadine, or sweetened cranberry juice
- Prosecco, to top

1. Add the rosé and vodka to a cocktail shaker and shake.

2. Serve the cocktail on ice in a white wineglass.

3. Add a splash of pomegranate juice, grenadine, or sweetened cranberry juice.

4. Top with prosecco, then garnish with cherries or an orange slice.

PURPLE MARTIN

The Ocean House's little-sister property, the Weekapaug Inn, over-looks Quonochontaug Pond, just off the Atlantic Ocean. And whereas the big sister welcomes you with lush grandiosity, the Weeka-paug exudes cozy charm. Built in 1899, then rebuilt after the Hurri-cane of 1938, all efforts have been made to preserve the inn's quaint historic character. And few drinks can make you feel right at home in such mellow luxury as this fizzy botanical sipper.

GLASSWARE: Champagne flute

GARNISH: Thyme sprig; lemon wheel, thinly sliced

- 1½ oz. Empress 1908 Gin
- 1½ oz. soda water
- 1 oz. simple syrup
- 1 oz. freshly squeezed lemon juice
- 1 teaspoon thyme tincture

1. Add all of the ingredients to a cocktail shaker with ice and shake.

2. Strain the cocktail into a Champagne flute.

3. Garnish with a thyme sprig and a thinly sliced lemon wheel.

VERMONT

FREDDIE'S CHUTE

THANKS, IT HAS POCKETS

NEON GOD

NORTHSIDE

PANACHE

NO. 14 MAPLE OLD FASHIONED

To many people inside and outside the region, Vermont is the postcard-perfect state, one that comes with quaint villages, brilliant fall foliage, ski mountains, and scenic farms. As if that all weren't enough to sate any traveler's need for a pure dose of New England aesthetics, the state has become world-famous for its artisanal food and drink, from dairies producing ice creams and fine cheeses to distilleries and microbreweries that draw gourmet tourists and tipplers from around the world. And Vermont also boasts one of the region's most lively little cities in Burlington, a college town hugging the miraculously beautiful Lake Champlain. It's high up in the northwest part of the state, but on your way there, you might as well visit the state's other lovely towns, where stopping by a bar on a snowy evening makes for warm memories.

APRÈS COCKTAIL + WINE

2038 MOUNTAIN ROAD, STOWE

The building certainly seems an unlikely home for one of the Green Mountain State's most innovative cocktail lounges, so unassuming and incongruous that it's easily missed as you're driving up Mountain Road past the village of Stowe and the byroads to its many ski lodges. In fact, the converted 1840s farmhouse is best known as the local outpost of the Burlington-based day spa Mirror Mirror. When you walk in, the luxury skin care retail store is on the left, the hair salon is to the right, and spa treatment rooms are upstairs. And right in the center is Après, the cozy cocktail playland of Chris Leighton.

During the height of winter, the bar opens as early as 12:30 p.m. to serve drinks and small plates to spa clients and weary skiers coming down from the slopes. Summer is just as busy, but even though he opens later in the slower seasons of early spring and late fall, his flourishing local clientele still packs the lounge's twenty-five seats. Whatever time of year, the lounge really gets hopping after 6 p.m., when Mirror Mirror closes its part of the building. Then customers settle into

couches and on stools, and Leighton is there behind the bar, using and explaining all of the tools he's learned over the years, from clarified fresh juices and carbonations to unusual ingredients like watermelon radish. Meanwhile, his two assistants not only help with the charcuterie and snacks, but also in the "cocktail kitchen," coming up with infusions and syrups for Leighton's creations. "People who seek us out are cocktail nerds," Leighton says. "And even if much of what I do is things you can't do easily at home, that's what they like to talk about."

A native of Ellsworth, Maine, Leighton went to Husson College in Bangor with the intention of majoring in physical therapy. While in school, he worked as a medical assistant at Mount Desert Hospital in Bar Harbor, but he also spent time in that resort town's bar scene and became fascinated by bartending. "It's not an easy place to get a foot in," he says. "Bartenders in Bar Harbor have been bartenders forever, so there's not a ton of opportunity for newbies to advance." But Chris Heaton, owner of the once-popular nightlife spot Carmen Verandah, offered Leighton a deal: "I'll teach you the cocktail craft here as long as you man the door on our dance-club nights . . . for a year." By the time Leighton graduated from Husson in 2013, he had switched to a business degree with a minor in entrepreneurship.

Postcollege, Leighton moved to Vermont, settled in at restaurants in Burlington, then worked at Caledonia Spirits' Barr Hill distillery in Montpelier (see page 340), where he learned about the same innovative ingredients and techniques that he still uses today. While there, his sister was working as a massage therapist at Mirror Mirror in Burlington, and she told him how the business was looking to create a cocktail lounge in its new Stowe location. They offered him the chance to own it, and while the location was unusual, Leighton knew from his education and his experiences that owning his own bar was a rare opportunity for a young cocktail nerd like himself.

Après opened in November 2021, and has grown rapidly, just by word of mouth—"I've spent about $20 on marketing," Leighton laughs—and thanks to hotel concierges in Stowe, who continue to send customers his way, customers who just want to taste something new and high-concept up in the heart of Vermont's ski country. "Vermont is very beer oriented, and Stowe is in particular," Leighton says, pointing out that the world-famous microbrewery The Alchemist is his neighbor. "I think we've thrown a wrench into things by creating something that's really good here that's not beer. That being said, I'm not changing the world or being too serious; I'm just trying to give people something they can enjoy that makes their day better, that they can relax with."

FREDDIE'S CHUTE

APRÈS COCKTAIL + WINE

2038 MOUNTAIN ROAD, STOWE

Over at the nearby ski slopes of Stowe Mountain Resort, there's a short but steep black-diamond trail called Freddie's Chute, which drops you almost 200 feet in less than a quarter mile. If you can manage that thrill ride, then you can manage this thrilling blend of spicy jalapeño, smoky mezcal, and citrus juices.

&

GLASSWARE: Rocks glass

GARNISH: Grapefruit slice, jalapeño slice

- 1½ oz. silver tequila
- 1½ oz. fresh grapefruit juice
- ¾ oz. jalapeño-infused Vermont maple syrup
- ½ oz. mezcal
- ½ oz. fresh lime juice

1. Add all of the ingredients to a cocktail shaker with ice and shake.

2. Strain the cocktail into a rocks glass over new ice.

3. Garnish with a slice of grapefruit and a slice of jalapeño.

THANKS, IT HAS POCKETS

APRÈS COCKTAIL + WINE

2038 MOUNTAIN ROAD, STOWE

Among all of Vermont's bold local microbrews and whiskeys, this cocktail of delicate flavors has to be in the upper echelon of what the Green Mountain State has to offer. With Barr Hill's gin made from wildflower honey, the orange blossom water, and the aromatized aperitif wine Lillet Blanc, this drink is a bounty of botanicals.

GLASSWARE: Nick & Nora glass, chilled

GARNISH: Lime zest/Luxardo cherry "flag"

- 1½ oz. Barr Hill Gin
- 1 oz. orange blossom water
- ¾ oz. clarified lime juice
- ½ oz. Lillet Blanc
- ½ oz. simple syrup

1. Add all of the ingredients to a mixing glass and stir.

2. Pour the cocktail into a chilled Nick & Nora glass.

3. Garnish with a lime zest/Luxardo cherry "flag."

NEON GOD

The Archives is such a vibrant, unique bar that one location can't contain it. There is one Archives in the bustling college town of Burlington, and another in nearby Winooski, which has recently become Vermont's latest hot spot for nightlife. Featuring local craft beers from a state that has some of the most lauded microbreweries in the country, The Archives also has classic and new cocktails—and vintage arcade games. Yes, you can be slugging down a dark lager from von Trapp Brewing or this cocktail while playing *Asteroids, Galaga, Mortal Kombat II, NBA Jam,* and, of course, *Pac-Man.* If the Neon God sounds like a video game . . . well, the name for this brightly colored Daiquiri actually comes from the Simon & Garfunkel song "The Sounds of Silence." Beverage director Sean McKenzie explains that he likes the evocative line in the song, which provided a cool image for this spirit-forward, aromatic cocktail that's anchored by a split base of full-flavored higher-proof rums.

ॐ

GLASSWARE: Double old-fashioned glass, chilled

- 1½ oz. Rhum J.M Blanc 50% ABV
- 1 oz. pineapple juice
- ½ oz. lime juice
- ½ oz. vanilla syrup
- ¼ oz. Smith & Cross Jamaica Rum
- ¼ oz. Amaro Montenegro

2. Double-strain the cocktail over a large rock into a chilled double old-fashioned glass.

NORTHSIDE

THE 126
126 COLLEGE STREET, BURLINGTON

Located down the street from the University of Vermont, The 126 is a hub of activity, with its 1920s-style bar and live music at least four nights a week. "We highlight classics from pre-1929," says The 126's Emily Morton, who won the United States Bartenders' Guild's award for Best Vermont Bartender of the Year in 2019. "Nearly all of our house cocktails contain sherry, brandy, port, liqueurs used back then, or fortified wine." For this cocktail, she put a twist on the traditional Southside cocktail, by bringing more complexity and brightness to a drink that is mainly gin, lime, and mint. She added fino sherry and grapefruit juice, and thus created a fan favorite.

— ॐ —

GLASSWARE: Nick & Nora glass
GARNISH: Mint leaf

- 2 oz. Beefeater Gin
- ¾ oz. Lustau Fino Jarana Sherry
- ¾ oz. fresh grapefruit juice
- ½ oz. fresh lime juice
- ½ oz. simple syrup (1:1)
- 5 large mint leaves

1. Combine all of the ingredients in a shaker.

2. Add dense ice and shake vigorously.

3. Double-strain the cocktail into a Nick & Nora.

4. Garnish with a fresh mint leaf.

PANACHE

One of the oldest continuously operating restaurants in Burlington, Leunig's has the panache of an elegant French bistro and is poised at the corner of Church and College streets, right on the Church Street Marketplace, the four-block pedestrian-only thoroughfare. Leunig's boasts a fine cocktail program, featuring many French spirits and liqueurs like absinthe, yellow and green Chartreuse, and Courvoisier. But for the Panache, bartender Matt Grant chose a simple, elegant beverage, true to the style of Leunig's itself, which he says is perfect for sipping on their patio on a warm day, as you let people—and time—pass by.

GLASSWARE: Wineglass

GARNISH: Lemon twist

- 1 oz. Yellow Chartreuse
- ½ oz. honey syrup (1:1)
- Club soda, to top

1. Build the ingredients, except the club soda, in a wineglass filled with ice.

2. Top with club soda and stir the ingredients with a barspoon.

3. Garnish with a twist of lemon.

NO. 14 MAPLE OLD FASHIONED

WOODSTOCK INN & RESORT
14 THE GREEN, WOODSTOCK

When people think of that quintessential New England village, they may not realize that they're visualizing Woodstock, Vermont. Not only do you have a pretty town with historic buildings galore, but you also have countless activities for all four seasons, from horseback riding to skiing to fishing to exploring the copious arts and crafts on the main street or on nearby back roads. At the center of it all is the Woodstock Inn & Resort, with its broad green lawn and its setting adjacent to the Marsh-Billings-Rockefeller National Historical Park. Not only is it a lovely place to stay, but also to relax with a drink, like this Vermont take on an all-time classic, using a local distiller's bourbon that softens the strong spirit with the unofficial flavor of the entire state: maple.

GLASSWARE: Rocks glass

- Splash soda water
- Luxardo cherry
- Orange slice
- 2 dashes Angostura bitters
- 2½ oz. Vermont Spirits No. 14 Maple Bourbon

1. Add a splash of soda water to a rocks glass.

2. Muddle the Luxardo cherry and orange slice in the bottom of the glass.

3. Fill the glass with ice.

4. Add the bitters, then the bourbon, and stir.

SPIRIT ARTISANS

HARTFORD FLAVOR COMPANY

WESTFORD HILL DISTILLERS

LIQUID RIOT BOTTLING CO.

SWEETGRASS WINERY & DISTILLERY

BEAVER POND DISTILLERY

BULLY BOY DISTILLERS

COPPER CANNON DISTILLERY

TAMWORTH DISTILLING

THE INDUSTRIOUS SPIRIT COMPANY

NEWPORT CRAFT BREWING + DISTILLING CO.

CALEDONIA SPIRITS

VERMONT DISTILLERS

New England has the longest history of distilling in the country, beginning with the early colonists making their own alcoholic drinks with their own apple cider and rum. The phenomenon of "craft distilling" as we know it today, however, has only been around for the past couple decades. But once that trend took off, it quickly became clear that this region is tailor-made for entrepreneurs of all ages and backgrounds to produce fine gins, rums, whiskeys, and liqueurs.

Each one of the distillers profiled in this section has a keen artisanal focus on making the best possible spirits, of course, but also on doing so in a way that's environmentally sustainable. Whether they're based on a farm, in the woods, or in the city, they pride themselves on supporting local farmers who make their businesses possible. Even more, they all have pride in their communities, and aim to create a welcoming atmosphere in their tasting rooms and restaurants. So when you're hitting the road around New England's six states, be sure to stop by any one of these distillers to say hello and raise a glass.

HARTFORD FLAVOR COMPANY

30 ARBOR STREET, HARTFORD, HARTFORDFLAVOR.COM

It's a true and unusual fact that one of New England's most distinctive distilleries exists as a direct result of a series of allergic reactions. In the early 2010s, Lelaneia Dubay was an artist, landscape designer, and herbalist who enjoyed making her own cranberry liqueur as a Christmas gift for friends. But then she not only developed gluten intolerance, but chemical intolerance, where certain additives would trigger headaches and other painful symptoms. She ruefully decided to detox her body and not drink for months, but that came with its own problems. "Life sucks without a cocktail," she says bluntly.

But then she considered the cranberry liqueur: she knew what was in it, as it didn't have any artificial colors or flavors that would make her sick, so she made some more and added a batch of lavender liqueur, using the flowers in her garden. She brought the liqueurs to a holiday party in 2013 that happened to be attended by various Hartford-area mixologists and restaurant owners, and the booze was a smash hit. "They said it was 'magic in a bottle' and that I had to get it into market, but I didn't want to work that hard on it," Dubay says, laughing. "But my husband, Tom, was quite interested in getting it going too." And if that didn't spur her enough, she tried going out and having a regular cocktail in a bar, her first in a year. She soon had a crippling headache again, and her night was ruined.

"I thought to myself, 'If I don't do this, I won't be able to have a cocktail out again,'" Dubay explains. "My scheme was to make these liqueurs and have them in cocktails out everywhere I can, so I can drink! I never would have done this at all without that intolerance, so here I am, running a woman-owned, organic, garden-to-glass distillery, working on bringing flavor to our world in cocktails."

Come 2014, she went into her kitchen and made fifty flavors, whittled them down to sixteen, and then had a panel of 300 people test

the flavors. When they launched the Hartford Flavor Company in March 2015, the first products were five Wild Moon liqueurs: rose, cucumber, lavender, birch, and chai spice, followed by cranberry when those tart red fruits became available in the fall. These were the flavors that tested well and were marketable for being somewhat familiar (but also just a bit unusual) and local in inspiration. The birch liqueur, for example, is made from the bark of white birch trees, but the idea came from Dubay's love of Foxon Park White Birch Soda, made in East Haven—Dubay grew up drinking it while chowing down slices from New Haven's world-famous pizzerias. (Full disclosure: this New Haven–native author can testify that this combo is simply the best.) And now Hartford Flavor Company has branched out by also producing organic and vanilla vodkas.

But all the while, Dubay stays quite aware of the history and beneficial aspects of where her products come from. For one, she sources her ingredients at home or as close to home as possible. The lavender and sage she uses come from her own garden, the cucumbers from six miles away in nearby Glastonbury, and the cranberries from Cape

Cod—using extra berries to concentrate the red color—so that it is all-natural and additive free, and for Dubay, this is a standard to which we should all return.

"We've lost so much of that culture, where we really knew about plants and their properties—those centuries of making tinctures where nature has given us these plants as our medicines," she says. "It's an age-old idea. I am a plants woman, and what I am doing is trying to capture that spirit of the plant by taking the life force of the plant and transferring it to the alcohol, which then becomes a component of a twenty-first-century cocktail. That's magic to me."

BIRCH & BOURBON

HARTFORD FLAVOR COMPANY

30 ARBOR STREET, HARTFORD

The local Foxon Park White Birch Soda is such an iconic fixture in southern Connecticut, especially when paired with a slice or three from one of New Haven's world-famous pizzerias. Hartford Flavor Company takes the birch's rootsy sweetness and pairs it with alcohol, both in its own liqueur and then with bourbon. But hell, get the pizza anyway.

GLASSWARE: Large lowball glass

GARNISH: Birch stick, orange peel

- 2 oz. bourbon
- 1 oz. Wild Moon Birch Liqueur

1. In a large lowball glass, pour the ingredients over a large ice cube.

2. Stir well and garnish with a birch stick and an orange peel.

THE LAVENDER LEMONADE

HARTFORD FLAVOR COMPANY

30 ARBOR STREET, HARTFORD

If the prior cocktail from the Hartford Flavor Company shows off the dark-liquor earthiness of its products, this one highlights its bright floral aspects through the use of lavender, which is one of the garden ingredients that spurred the idea for the company in the first place.

GLASSWARE: Collins glass

GARNISH: Lemon peel or lavender flowers

- 3 oz. lemonade
- 1 oz. Wild Moon Lavender Liqueur
- 1 oz. Hartford Flavor Company Organic Vodka
- ¼ oz. fresh lemon juice

1. Add all of the ingredients to a shaker with ice and shake.

2. Pour the cocktail into a collins glass.

3. Garnish with a lemon peel or lavender flowers.

WESTFORD HILL DISTILLERS

196 CHATEY ROAD, ASHFORD, WESTFORDHILL.COM

Even in a region so rich with history, Louis and Margaret Chatey of Westford Hill Distillers can boast a distinctly lengthy pedigree. Located deep in the heart of the wooded, quiet northeastern corner of Connecticut, the distillery was created on land settled by a subsistence farmer named Thomas Peake in 1711. When Charles Chatey purchased the property in 1919, he was its fifth owner. And now his grandson Louis and Louis's wife, Margaret, are producing some of the country's finest eaux-de-vie and other spirits on the farm, and they've become a landmark themselves. When they founded their company in 1995 and got licensed in 1998, they were among the first six craft distillers in the United States, and the only one east of the Rocky Mountains. But they got started long before then.

"I came back here after college, and I started planting wine grapes in the early 1980s," Louis says. "That's the era when people were learning all about good wine, and little wineries were getting going." He was already learning all about the wine business in California, working in sales for such heavy hitters as Sebastiani, Diageo, and Constellation.

He switched gears when the couple was traveling in the Alsace region of France. A local winemaker there invited them in and poured them a glass of framboise eau-de-vie, a clear unaged brandy bearing the aromatic flavor of raspberry. Immediately they were converted, and they saw the opportunity to use local fruits in their New England backyard, but they wondered why they weren't seeing these sublime spirits in the United States.

"Coming from a wine background," Louis says, "I completely responded to how the idea of terroir—how the land influences the wine—could apply to spirits. After all, brandy making is like wine making, in that you have the inherent quality of the fruit specific to the land."

Enter Jörg Rupf, founder of St. George Spirits in California, and for years in the 1980s, the only eau-de-vie producer in the United States. A German expat, Rupf is considered a crucial pioneer of craft distilling, often credited with helping get federal legislation passed that would allow artisanal alcohol producing companies in the first place. He was also evangelistic about the distilling techniques and equipment that he brought over from Europe, so when Louis Chatey contacted Rupf, a mentorship began.

"Jörg was generous with his time, but at first, he would vet you," Louis says. "He would make sure how serious you are, as he didn't want to work with anyone who would be producing anything less than the optimum. He helped us get a still from Germany, and he worked

with us out here, teaching us many things about the process, and if we had any issue after that, he was always on the other end of the phone. And the focus was always the idea of establishing character in your spirits. If someone tastes something from Westford Hill, it has a signature to it; you know it's from here."

Westford Hill produces a variety of eaux-de-vie, familiar to any Europhile gastronome: their own framboise, as well as pear William, fraise (strawberry), and a German kirsch (cherry). They have expanded their product line to include organic vodka, rum, gin, and vermouth, and, being New Englanders, of course they make apple brandy, but apples' longevity means that they can make a version that has been aged for twenty-one years.

"Back when we were getting started, I would go to wine shops and restaurants, and there wasn't much understanding of how a spirit was really made," says Margaret, who handles the sales and marketing side of the business. "And this was before the whole locavore movement. A key part of our business was supporting local farmers who were growing amazing fruit, and turning it into our product. Not only did the movement catch up to us, but we also have the advantage of a newer generation discovering cocktails and leaning into them. Cocktails have reemerged in a big way, and I like to think in part that's because there are more interesting craft spirits to play with."

The Chateys and Westford Hill have made best-of lists in magazines like *Bon Appétit* and have also won competitions in the United States and Europe, including earning Eau-de-Vie of the Year at the Berlin International Spirits Competition. In 2015, the Smithsonian Institution chose Westford Hill to represent craft distillation in its History of Food series. "That's the highest honor we've ever received," Louis says.

But the Chateys do not rest on their laurels. After twenty years in business, Westford Hill could finally welcome visitors and sell their wares at the farm, thanks to a change in Connecticut state law, so the couple has enjoyed this new way to meet customers and educate them while giving them a place to picnic while enjoying a lovely eau-de-vie. As for Louis, his own education is never-ending: "From a distiller's point of view, we're starting to learn what we don't know, then just continuing to experiment and expand into other things that we might try. Distilling in this country is still so much in its infancy, but it's all just a tremendous opportunity that lies ahead of us. That's what keeps me going."

GOVERNOR'S CUP

WESTFORD HILL DISTILLERS
196 CHATEY ROAD, ASHFORD

Among the distillery's many honors is Westford Hill's creation of this cocktail for the inaugural ball of Connecticut governor Ned Lamont. This drink includes their vodka, which serves to brighten the brandy and make it pop even more amid the fruit juices.

—— 🕭 ——

GLASSWARE: Rocks glass

GARNISH: Apple slice

- 2 oz. Westford Hill Distillers Organic Rime Vodka
- 2 oz. cranberry juice
- 2 oz. pomegranate juice
- 1 oz. Westford Hill Distillers New World Aged Apple Brandy
- Dash key lime juice

1. Combine all of the ingredients in a shaker with ice and shake.

2. Pour the cocktail into a rocks glass. Garnish with slice of apple.

SWEET & SAVORY PEAR

WESTFORD HILL DISTILLERS
196 CHATEY ROAD, ASHFORD

Anchored by the evanescent flavors of Westford Hill's Pear William, this cocktail also boasts aromatic touches of cucumber, basil, and ginger to create a drink both light and complex.

—————————— ∞ ——————————

GLASSWARE: Martini glass
GARNISH: Fresh basil leaf, cucumber slice

- 1 teaspoon grated fresh ginger
- 2 tablespoons simple syrup
- 3 inches fresh cucumber, peeled, seeded, and diced

- 2 basil leaves, torn
- 1 tablespoon fresh lime juice
- 2 oz. Westford Hill Distillers Pear William Eau-de-Vie

1. Press the grated ginger through a garlic press or fine strainer to release the juice into the simple syrup.

2. In a cocktail shaker, muddle the diced cucumber and basil leaves.

3. Add the ginger syrup, lime juice, ice, and Pear William.

4. Pour the cocktail into a martini glass and garnish with a fresh basil leaf and a slice of cucumber.

LIQUID RIOT BOTTLING CO.

250 COMMERCIAL STREET, PORTLAND, LIQUIDRIOT.COM

Back in 2008, Eric and Julie Michaud surprised the Portland restaurant and nightlife scene with Novare Res Bier Café, which instantly became the city's premier palace of beer, boasting bottles, cans, and drafts from all over New England, North America, and Europe. Eric Michaud had studied sake brewing in Japan and learned beer brewing techniques from Trappist monks in Belgium, so the couple took this knowledge, plus a passion for arcane brews, and opened this beer bar with a Latin name that means, "To start a revolution." The name was meant to evoke the urge for people to commune together and discuss making the world a better place, but also to stake out a renewed focus on craft beers and small producers. Novare Res is still a mecca for beer lovers today, but by 2013, the Michauds were ready to raise a new ruckus in the town's drinking scene.

Enter Liquid Riot. In this case, the name is inspired by two events in 1855: the Chicago Lager Beer Riot, caused when the Windy City mayor at the time tried to close taverns on Sundays; and, closer to home, the Portland Rum Riot, caused when the port city's mayor tried to enforce an alcohol ban by hoarding $1,600 worth of rum in city hall. The name for the new business was fitting for one that would brew its own beers and distill its own spirits.

The phrase Liquid Riot uses is "a twisting continuous loop," in reference to the company's cross-utilization of products from the brewery and the distillery. "That's the infinity fermentation," says Matthew Marrier, Liquid Riot vice president of operations. "Everything is being used infinitely, internally, in-house. We recycle our water. All of our spent grains go to the farms, which feeds the animals, and we buy the meat from the farms. The byproducts of our beer get distilled the traditional German way into our bierschnaps—no beer goes to waste. Everything is being used in a big loop."

Liquid Riot's focus on tradition is also consistent across both brewery and distillery. Their beers contain no trendy, quirky ingredients like doughnuts or lactosugar, while the bourbon is made with a traditional build of fifty-one percent corn. And all of the corn, wheat, and malts that go into Liquid Riot's spirits are grown in Maine. "Our goal is to be one hundred percent local," Marrier says, "and we'd like to grow more ourselves. Our head distiller has been cultivating property with cherry and peach trees. Our brewer is doing the same thing: planting seeds. And with our cocktail program at the restaurant, we try to source everything from the summer local harvest as much as we can. We've given farmers a list of everything we want for our cocktail program and our kitchen."

All this would be merely well and noble if the beers weren't delicious, both complex and refreshing, and if their spirits didn't keep winning silvers and golds at marquee events like the San Francisco World Spirits Competition—for a taste of Liquid Riot's victory, check out the Old Port Bourbon Whiskey, the Fernet Michaud Digestif, and a collaboration with Sebago Brewing called Bonfire Spirit. And if you want a taste of some history, be sure to snatch up an annual bottle of the Rum Riot Rum, a collaboration with Maine Craft Distilling and New England Distilling. Every year on June 2, the anniversary of their city's notorious boozy brouhaha, they combine elements of each of their own recipes into one barrel, which they let age for years. But they also tap a barrel of this dark rum that's now finished nicely, and they raise a glass to their forebears who once fought for their right to raise it.

FRENCH FINCH PUNCH

LIQUID RIOT BOTTLING CO.

250 COMMERCIAL STREET, PORTLAND

This cocktail is herbal and spicy," says Matthew Marrier, Liquid Riot vice president of operations, "but not overwhelming from the fernet and ginger. They really complement each other. The combination of the dry gin and lime lends well to balance the sweetness from the lemongrass syrup."

❧

GLASSWARE: Nick & Nora glass, chilled

GARNISH: Mint leaves, freshly grated nutmeg

- 1 oz. Liquid Riot Fernet Michaud
- ½ oz. Martell Cognac VS
- ½ oz. London dry gin
- ½ oz. ginger-lime syrup
- ½ oz. fresh lime juice
- ¼ oz. lemongrass syrup

1. Combine all of the ingredients in a shaker tin.

2. Add a generous amount of ice and shake vigorously until the tin is nice and frosty.

3. Double-strain the cocktail into a chilled Nick & Nora glass.

4. For the garnish, smack fresh mint leaves and place them gently on the rim of the glass, then add a very small amount of freshly grated nutmeg.

CONGRESS STREET CURE

LIQUID RIOT BOTTLING CO.
250 COMMERCIAL STREET, PORTLAND

I f Portland were a Caribbean island, this is what the national drink would be," Matthew Marrier says. "Blackberries play a big part in this fun and fruity cocktail that is not overly sweet and not overly boozy. It is a blast of blackberry up front on the palate, with a little lemon zip on the back end to give it balance. The bierschnaps gives a unique aroma of hops. I love to use Vena's Fizz House Maine Pine Bitters to give an essence of the wooded lands of Maine."

GLASSWARE: Hurricane glass

GARNISH: Edible flowers, blackberries

- 1 oz. Liquid Riot Portland Rum Riot Rum
- 1 oz. Liquid Riot Bierschnaps
- 1 oz. falernum
- 1 oz. blackberry puree
- ¾ oz. fresh lemon juice
- ½ oz. agave simple syrup
- 4 to 5 dashes Vena's Fizz House Maine Pine Bitters

1. Combine all of the ingredients in a shaker tin, then add a generous amount of ice and shake vigorously, until the tin is nice and frosty.

2. Strain the cocktail into a hurricane glass over crushed ice.

3. Top with more crushed ice. Garnish with edible flowers of your choice and blackberries.

SWEETGRASS WINERY & DISTILLERY

347 CARROLL ROAD, UNION, AND 324 FORE STREET,
PORTLAND, SWEETGRASSWINERY.COM

A satisfying part of tracking down one of the best gins in New England is the road trip to the farm that the distillery calls home. First, you need to make your way up to Midcoast Maine, which is a popular destination anyway, thanks to the well-touristed harbor towns on U.S. Route 1, like Camden and Rockland. But now you need to turn inland on State Route 17 and head for the farm town of Union. After about 20 minutes, you hang a right on Shepard Hill Road and go up and down hills and through farms and forest, then take another right on the even more narrow and verdant Carroll Road—if you cross the brook, you've missed the turn. Go up the steep hill of Carroll Road, and there on the left is the Sweetgrass headquarters, clad in weathered shingles, with the signs "WINERY" and "DISTILLERY" assuring you that you actually did get here from there.

Walk around the building and you'll find a gorgeous hillside porch, and inside you'll find Keith and Constance Bodine selling gorgeous liquors. Though Constance grew up in a military family, her mother was from the Boothbay area down the coast, and with a childhood of regular visits, she considered Maine a kind of home base her whole life. "And I was familiar with Union growing up," Constance says. "My father carved birds for the Union Fair exhibit hall, and when Keith and I got married, we purchased a sideboard in the antique store there. So when we wanted to move closer to family, we knew we wouldn't get the space we wanted in Boothbay, so we came up here. As soon as we saw this place, and its beautiful view, we knew. It's a way off Route 1, but who wants to live near Route 1?"

That was the year 2005, and the Bodines had taken a circuitous path to get there. Back in the 1980s, they met at the New Mexico

Institute of Mining and Technology, where Keith was earning a bachelor's degree in computer science and mathematics, while Constance was earning three math degrees. "But ever since I've known Keith, he's had an interest in wine and then in spirits," Constance says. "We were married and started our jobs in engineering, but he had a feeling he wanted to produce something that he loved. So after about ten years into our work, he went back to school for it." That school was the University of California, Davis, with its famous viticulture and enology department, and Keith earned his master's degree in food science there, writing his thesis on sensory analysis: how what you consume should taste and feel in your mouth. Working at various wineries here and abroad further expanded his knowledge base on what makes a spectacular drink, and how to make it.

And the spectacular drink that put Sweetgrass on distillery maps all over the world is its Back River Gin. Not only has *Forbes* magazine named it one of the best American gins, it has earned a 95 rating from *Wine Enthusiast*, which also listed it as one of the Top 50 spirits in the world. A London-style dry gin, it was the first product that Sweetgrass brought to market, and even today it wows everyone with its distinct and strong botanical richness. "Keith is all about flavor," Constance says. "That's why he doesn't make vodka—he wants what he makes to have a distinct taste and smell. This not a quiet, sit-on-the-shelf gin, but one that makes you take notice. He wanted bright flavors that would stand out, and the unusual botanical we use is wild Maine blueberries, which don't make the gin sweet when they're distilled, but rather give an earthy bogginess." The name of the gin refers to the estuary that flows through her beloved Boothbay: "Our gin really mimics the Back River, with the mud and pine air and the blueberry barrens. It really has the feel of being on that river." The taste is so distinctive, Sweetgrass's preferred recipes for the gin are the simple Gin & Tonic and a Martini, so that you don't obscure it too much.

But despite the fame of their flagship gin, Sweetgrass also excels at a wide variety of other liquors and fruit-based wines: a thirty-six-month-aged apple brandy; the smooth Three Crow Rum; vermouth; rhubarb and maple smashes; fortified wines made with cranberries and blueberries; apple and blueberry sangrias; and hard ciders. To produce all this, they use 70,000 lbs. of Maine-grown grain and fruit each year, getting wild blueberries and maple from as close as Union and as far as Washington County near the Canadian border. They get their apples from one town over, where an orchard has many old varieties of apples, some that don't even have a recorded name.

The Bodines have also added another tasting room, in downtown Portland, for those who might not make the lovely but lengthy trip up to the farm. "Usually when we come up with an idea, we both have to like it or it can't go forward," Constance says. "But once we create something we want to drink, the wonderful thing about owning a winery and distillery is that you're standing in a room with people who can give you feedback and ideas for where you could go next. Our younger customers have different tastes—which is why we offer sangrias and not the chardonnay of their grandmothers—and they're looking for a local experience, more tied to the area, and a great product that isn't the run-of-the-mill stuff that you get at the supermarket. With a new generation coming up, we get to experiment along with them."

BACK RIVER GIN & TONIC

SWEETGRASS WINERY & DISTILLERY

347 CARROLL ROAD,
UNION, AND 324 FORE STREET, PORTLAND

Thanks to customer feedback over the years, Constance Bodine estimates that ninety percent of Sweetgrass's customers drink their Back River Gin just like this: nice and simple. For the citrus fruit and juice, choose lemon, lime, or grapefruit.

&

GLASSWARE: Highball glass

GARNISH: Citrus wedge or slice

- 3 oz. Back River Gin
- ½ oz. freshly squeezed citrus juice
- 4 oz. tonic water

1. Fill a highball glass with ice, and add the gin and citrus juice.

2. Top with the tonic water.

3. Garnish with a wedge or slice of the citrus fruit of your choice.

NEW ENGLAND COCKTAILS — 289

THE MAINE MARTINI

SWEETGRASS WINERY & DISTILLERY
347 CARROLL ROAD,
UNION, AND 324 FORE STREET, PORTLAND

Though Sweetgrass's Back River Gin is always the glittering superstar of any cocktail, it blends smoothly with the distillery's sublime dry vermouth. Another simple cocktail, but with flavors as full as these, this is all you need.

GLASSWARE: Martini glass, chilled
GARNISH: Anchovy-stuffed olives

- 2 oz. Back River Gin
- 1 oz. Sweetgrass Vermouth
- Dash Sweetgrass Bitter Blueberry Bitters

1. Combine all of the ingredients in a mixing glass and fill the glass with ice.

2. Stir well to chill the mixture and strain the cocktail into a chilled martini glass.

3. Garnish with an anchovy-stuffed olive or two.

MA

BEAVER POND DISTILLERY

88 WOODWARD ROAD, PETERSHAM,
BEAVERPONDDISTILLERY.COM

Jerry Friedman had a problem, albeit one that most people would envy. After thirty years as an immigration attorney in Boston, he was finally taking down his shingle and retiring. He'd been interested in distilling for a long time, and he had been a home winemaker for years with friends—every fall he'd make wine with grapes purchased whole-sale at the New England Produce Market in Chelsea, a gritty little city nearby. One year he was moving all these cases of homemade wine around, and he realized that he could distill them down into a clear brandy called eau-de-vie. Pretty soon, that suburban backyard hobby took on a larger role in his life, and he moved operations west to a barn in the tiny Pioneer Valley town of Petersham, in central Massa-chusetts. "I practiced law for thirty years, and while the first twenty-nine were fun, that last year felt more like a sentence than a career," he says, laughing. "So I just said, 'Okay, life is short, you gotta start having fun.' So this is my retirement project, and while it's a challenge, it's definitely fun."

His passion for eaux-de-vie, however, dates back much further than that. When he was in his twenties, he was backpacking around rural France and came upon a distillery in the Pyrenees that made these un-sweetened, unaged, clear brandies. Made from various varieties of fruit, they are alcohol forward, with an evanescence of the fruit that brushes the palate in a singularly sublime fashion. "I saw a sign saying he was a distiller," Friedman says, "but when I went in for a tasting, he handed me something I'd never seen before, a pear eau-de-vie. It just blew me away. I'd never tasted anything like it before, and I've been chasing that taste ever since." In fact, over the many decades, he's also traveled to the former Yugoslavia, Austria, Germany, and

California, trying these indescribable "alcools" made with anything from plums to cherries to apples to apricots. "So then thirty years later, I'm buying distilling equipment from Germany and reconfiguring my barn, and there I am in business without knowing what I'm doing, or how much fruit I needed," Friedman says. "If somebody looked at it from the outside, they'd say it's a mistake. Somebody asked me, 'Why make these brandies?' And the answer it that I like them."

Though he gets occasional help from friends or his kids, Beaver Pond Distillery is basically a one-man show. Most of the fruit comes from this agricultural part of Massachusetts, though some stone fruits come from across the western border in New York State. He has a machine that, for example, will crush peaches and take the pits out. The raw mash has a consistency of applesauce, which then goes into drums with added yeast. Once fermentation is done, all the mash and the pulp go into a fifty-gallon still designed specifically for brandy production. Just the ethanol middle alcohols, known in distilling parlance as the "hearts," go into storage in stainless steel containers to mellow and be brought down to 80 proof by adding water over a period of months. "When it's at the appropriate proof, I put a label on a bottle, and that's the product," Friedman says. "The process takes about six to eight months, but bringing it down to proof might take an extra month. I don't have temperature-controlled fermentation. The process I have here is that I have enough heat in my barn to prevent the pipes from freezing, so I can control the temperature by opening and closing the door of the barn."

If this all sounds delightfully homespun, the sleekly polished finished product is anything but. His eaux-de-vie are available at many select liquor stores around Massachusetts and by appointment at the distillery itself. Any curious tippler or eau-de-vie enthusiast will find that the Beaver Pond spirits indeed have that ineffable spirit of the fruits hovering over the strong alcohol base. They mix wonderfully with cocktails or are delicious on their own. This author is partial to Beaver Pond's version of slivovitz (or slivovice), that classic Eastern European brandy made from damson plums, especially when chilled and served in a snifter that focuses its bouquet. But Friedman says he's just happy kicking back by his barn with any of his eaux-de-vie in an old jelly jar, and frankly, it's impossible to top that.

GIN BLOSSOM

BEAVER POND DISTILLERY

88 WOODWARD ROAD, PETERSHAM

Lonnie Newburn of The Boston Shaker (see page 27) helped compile this recipe and the next for Beaver Pond Distillery. Most common eaux-de-vie are made from pear or raspberries, but this one features the unusual (and unusually delicious) apricot eau-de-vie.

— ❧ —

GLASSWARE: Coupe glass or jelly jar

GARNISH: Orange peel

- 1½ oz. gin
- 1½ oz. blanco vermouth
- ¾ oz. Beaver Pond Distillery Apricot Eau de Vie
- Dash orange bitters

1. Add all of the ingredients to a mixing glass and stir.

2. Pour the cocktail into a coupe or jelly jar.

3. Garnish with an orange peel.

CHERRY AVIATION

BEAVER POND DISTILLERY
88 WOODWARD ROAD, PETERSHAM

With its purple hue and almost frothy, floral fruitiness, the Aviation is a singularly beautiful cocktail. But now it's made even more dreamy with a strong dose of Beaver Pond's cherry brandy.

&⃝

GLASSWARE: Coupe glass or jelly jar

GARNISH: Lemon peel

- 2 oz. Beaver Pond Distillery Cherry Brandy Eau de Vie
- ¾ oz. lemon juice
- ¼ oz. maraschino liqueur
- 1 tablespoon crème de violette

1. Add all of the ingredients to a mixing glass and stir.

2. Pour the cocktail into a coupe or jelly jar.

3. Garnish with a lemon peel.

BULLY BOY DISTILLERS

44 CEDRIC STREET, ROXBURY,
BULLYBOYDISTILLERS.COM

Once upon a time, the Willis brothers—Dave and Will—were adventurous young boys growing up on their family's fourth-generation working farm, called Charlescote, in the wooded Boston suburb of Sherborn. They tended the livestock and worked the orchards and fields, and Dave remembers opening his first ice-cream stand at age 8. Their adventures would sometimes lead to the farmhouse's fieldstone basement, sealed by a thick steel door that their grandfather had salvaged from a bank vault. They played hide-and-seek down there, but as they hit their teenage years and started making hard cider from the farm's apples, they realized that the basement was a treasure trove of old pre-Prohibition and Prohibition-era spirits with labels like "cow whiskey" and "Medford rum." And amid this dusty collection was a framed picture of a beloved draft horse, honored as being "a willing and patient family instructor." The horse, Bully Boy, had worked the farm in the early 1900s and was named after the word "bully"—meaning "great" or "extraordinary"—coined by their great-grandfather's college friend, President Teddy Roosevelt. "At the time, we just didn't understand the magnitude of this discovery," says Dave Willis.

But by the mid-2000s, when the brothers were in their late twenties, the concept all came together. After their hard-cider years, they had been experimenting with distilling apple brandy, and then whiskey and rum in a small home still. By 2009, they decided to distill full-time, but they wanted to do it in the city of Boston, which had not been home to a major distillery since the old Mr. Boston plant closed in 1986. "Most distilleries were opening up in rural parts of the country," Dave says, "but with Boston's rich history—at one point it was the epicenter of rum distillation—we wanted to be part of that lin-

eage. The challenge was that no one knew what to do with us. We had to keep explaining that we were not a brewery, but a distillery."

Still, they found Boston officials receptive to the idea, and they opened up shop in 2010, with a focus on freshly produced liquors like vodka, white rum, and unaged whiskey. The state of Massachusetts offers Farmer Distillery licenses which allow producers to sell and distribute what they make, so Dave says they built industry buzz the old-fashioned way: "We'd pack up the car with vodka and drive around and sell it ourselves, rather than have a large distributor bury us under other brands. We built up enough of a book so we could then approach distributors from a position of strength. We went with Horizon Beverage, which was another old family business. That was a turning point for us: up until that point, if we wanted to sell vodka on Nantucket, it meant that I was driving to Hyannis on Cape Cod and putting it on a puddle jumper out to the islands, and somebody would have to get it on the other side. We would lose money on that. But now we could focus on the business of creating and scaling operations up."

These days, Bully Boy is one of the most established brands in New England. Now that they've been around for years, they offer aged whiskey and rum, as well as gin and amari. They have also developed a series of canned and bottled ready-made cocktails, ranging from Negroni and Manhattan to Grapefruit Spritz and Italian Iced Tea. "Our Old Fashioned has been out since 2016, but when COVID happened, it just supercharged all this stuff—everyone having to fend for themselves at home if they wanted a cocktail," Dave says. "But we were picky about it. We wanted to do cocktails that we could make with natural flavoring, ones that would be like those you could make at home."

The focus on all-natural and the home is carried over into how they source the grain for their liquors. Their effort to be as local as possible begins with Charlescote Farm, where they grow corn on eight acres and hope to expand to twenty acres. Then they send the grain to their cousin George Lewis, who owns Ventura Grain in Taunton and mills it into flour. Even when they have to supplement from other sources, the brothers always aim to give back to the place that grew them as well as the grain.

"Our main focus from a local and agricultural perspective is the corn," Dave says. "It's a commitment, not just to source locally, but sourcing from our family farm and figuring out how to pump money back into this small farm community in Massachusetts. That's our big story."

CRIMSON CLOVER

BULLY BOY DISTILLERS
44 CEDRIC STREET, ROXBURY

This cocktail highlights two of Bully Boy's major product lines: its base spirits like gin, and its amari, such as the Rabarbaro. Add a touch of frothy egg white, and it's guaranteed to highlight your evening.

ക്ക

GLASSWARE: Coupe glass

GARNISH: Sumac powder

- 1½ oz. Bully Boy Distillers Estate Gin
- ¼ oz. Bully Boy Distillers Amaro Rabarbaro
- 1 oz. lemon juice
- 1 oz. egg white
- 1 oz. Charlescote Concord Grape Syrup (see recipe)

1. Add all of the ingredients to a shaker and dry-shake, then shake with ice.

2. Strain the cocktail into a coupe.

3. Garnish with sumac powder.

CHARLESCOTE CONCORD GRAPE SYRUP: Blend 1 quart Concord grape juice, 1 quart sugar, and 1 oz. orange blossom water until all the sugar is dissolved. Depending on the season, you can replace the Concord grape juice with pomegranate juice.

WOODWARD

BULLY BOY DISTILLERS

44 CEDRIC STREET, ROXBURY

As you head into the cooler temperatures of the year, this cocktail brings you the comforting, warming scents and tastes of smoke and cinnamon and the charred oak of the barrels used in the American Straight Whiskey.

❧

GLASSWARE: Nick & Nora glass, wood smoked

GARNISH: Orange twist

- 2 oz. Bully Boy Distillers American Straight Whiskey
- ½ oz. Bully Boy Distillers Amaro
- ½ oz. Cinnamon Syrup (see recipe)

1. Add all of the ingredients to a mixing glass with ice and stir.

2. Strain the cocktail into a wood-smoked rocks glass.

3. Garnish with an orange twist.

CINNAMON SYRUP: Toast 5 cinnamon sticks in a pot. Add 1½ quarts water and 1½ quarts sugar. Bring the mixture to a simmer for 15 minutes. Let the syrup sit overnight in the refrigerator, then strain.

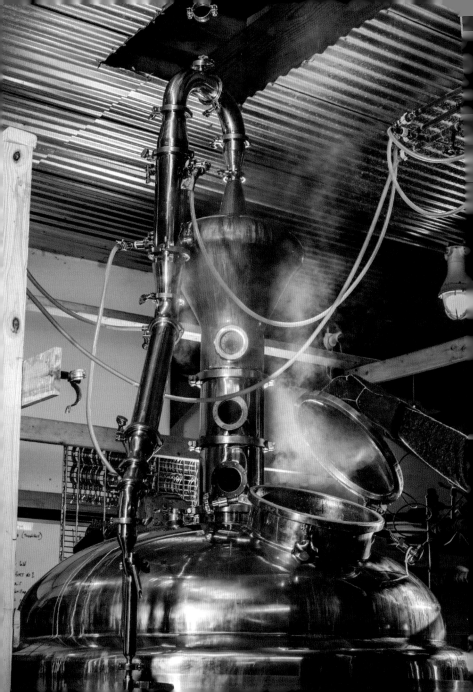

COPPER CANNON DISTILLERY

2 LYMAN WAY, WEST CHESTERFIELD,
COPPERCANNON.COM

Blake Amacker is unusual among the distillers in this book, in that he has no roots in New England, which of course is a region where its people, their histories, and their endeavors are anchored deep in the soil. Amacker is a transplant from Louisiana who graduated from Louisiana State University in 2004 with a bachelor's degree in mechanical engineering. Coming from one of the country's centers of petrochemical production, he knew that he could work in the oil fields but chose instead to work for the aerospace industry. A job beckoned in the Boston area, so he moved to New England's biggest and not always friendliest city to outsiders. Admittedly not "a super city person," Amacker moved to southeastern New Hampshire when a job opened up there, and now he is settled in, working for an international company as a sales engineer for electro-optical infrared systems.

Oh yes—he's also an award-winning distiller whose rums and bourbons are displayed proudly at his tasting room or in any of New Hampshire's state-run liquor stores. He first became interested in the craft when he and his cousin Chris Arnold flew to Ireland in 2010 before Arnold's wedding and found themselves visiting one distillery after another. Both of them were engineers, and with typical DIY attitudes, they figured they could make one themselves when they got home. After all, Amacker had been a homebrewer, and Arnold knew his spirits from working in bars. So Amacker built a home still in his garage, and its long copper cylinder reminded him of a huge potato gun. (A potato gun, for those unaware, is a homemade device beloved by Americans from many regions—including New England—where a long tube, lighter fluid, and an ignition combine to shoot tubers very long distances.) And that's how a vacation trip and a home experiment became a thriving business called Copper Cannon.

Amacker and Arnold created the company in 2013, but it didn't open until 2018. In that time, both of them immersed themselves in education. Arnold studied books on chemical engineering and process design, while Amacker volunteered at distilleries to get hands-on experience. They rebuilt an old barn from a nearby town that had been taken down when a Market Basket supermarket moved in. Though Arnold co-owns the business, he lives back in Houston, so Amacker set out doing the day-to-day distilling, starting with rums: a clear rum, an aged rum, a maple rum, and even that most New England concept, a pumpkin spice rum. "We take a bunch of different spices, pumpkin, and maple syrup, then steep it in our clear rum at high proof for a week or two," Amacker says. "We keep some of the debris in so you'll see the sediment, while the pumpkin turns it a shade of orange. But we filter it so that it doesn't get super sweet. Our stuff is on the alcohol-forward side, keeping it at 80 proof and not pushing it down to 60 or 40 proof." Copper Cannon has also branched into whiskey, with its Fort #1, a 101-proof rye bourbon that's aged in white oak for a minimum of two years and is released only four times a year, and a wheated bourbon in production.

"It's a hobby that kind of got out of control," Amacker admits. As a professional with a full-time job, and as a husband and father, he has the fortune of good help. His wife, Toni, handles the social media aspect of the business, and his sister Sara is a graphic designer who works at the LSU Museum of Art—she designed Copper Cannon's logo, labels, and branding. And he's no longer a one-man operation, thanks to the hire of distillery manager Jamie Berry, who also comes up with Copper Cannon's cocktails, including those in the following pages.

But Amacker has also done his part to help the burgeoning distilling industry in this northern state he's called home for more than fifteen years. As a member of the New Hampshire Craft Spirits Organization, he helped create a distillery trail that links all the businesses and markets them together for tourists. He'll host small events to get the word out about New Hampshire bourbon, and he'll welcome industry experts by cooking jambalaya for them.

"When we look around New Hampshire, the craft beer market is super saturated," Amacker says. "I mean, it's easy for people to just go drink a beer, while a cocktail requires a different mood. The distillery market is becoming busier, but it's not as saturated, so we need to keep pushing it into stores. I've always had this entrepreneurial spirit, and I like manufacturing processes in general. But this feels different—it's like cooking, and I really enjoy it. In a way, this distillery is my purpose."

PSYCHO KILLER

COPPER CANNON PREMIUM DISTILLERY

2 LYMAN WAY, WEST CHESTERFIELD

New Hampshire sure gets cold in the winter, and no matter how beautiful it can get in the ice and snow, Copper Cannon's Blake Amacker stays true to his Louisiana roots by disliking the season. Thankfully this tropical treat shares a few ingredients with the classic New Orleans Hurricane to help you forget about the blizzard outside.

GLASSWARE: Collins glass

GARNISH: Lemon wheel

- 2 oz. fresh orange juice
- 2 oz. fresh pineapple juice
- 1½ oz. Copper Cannon Hand-Crafted Barrel Aged Rum
- Splash grenadine
- Splash blue curaçao

1. Combine all of the ingredients, except the grenadine and blue curaçao, in a cocktail shaker and shake.

2. Strain the cocktail into a collins glass over fresh ice.

3. Add a splash of grenadine and a splash of blue curaçao to finish it off.

4. Garnish with a lemon wheel.

CANNON KIR

COPPER CANNON PREMIUM DISTILLERY

2 LYMAN WAY, WEST CHESTERFIELD

T hanks to the noble French, the Kir Royale has long been one of the simplest, most elegant cocktails to have before a meal. And with this variation, Copper Cannon's clear rum royally gives that Kir an extra kick.

ℬ

GLASSWARE: Nick & Nora glass

- 1¼ oz. Copper Cannon Hand-Crafted Clear Rum
- ½ oz. cassis liqueur
- Champagne, to top

1. Add the rum and cassis liqueur to a Nick & Nora glass, then top with Champagne.

NH

TAMWORTH DISTILLING

15 CLEVELAND HILL ROAD, TAMWORTH,
TAMWORTHDISTILLING.COM

At first, there were the brands. As the founder of the Philadelphia-based company Quaker City Mercantile, Steven Grasse had helped distillers turn their unnamed products into such world-famous brands as Hendrick's Gin and Sailor Jerry Rum, doing everything from naming and conceiving the identities for these spirits to designing the labels, bottles, and marketing campaigns. But by 2015, Grasse decided it was time to open up his own distillery, so he turned his attention toward New Hampshire, where he had bought a summer home and farm years before.

Tamworth is a picturesque town of some 3,000 people, nestled between the White Mountains National Forest to the north and the Lakes Region to the south. Along with Grasse, who is also a well-established writer of cocktail histories, other famous thought leaders over the past centuries who have summered there include William and Henry James, the poet E. E. Cummings, and even Grover Cleveland, the US president famously elected to two nonconsecutive terms.

This kind of creative community is reflected in Tamworth Distilling's constantly changing offerings. In addition to varieties of bourbons, rye whiskeys, brandies, and vodkas, the company also produces gins flavored naturally with ingredients like Thai chiles and spruce. Meanwhile, the cordials change all the time, depending on the availability and popularity of such diverse produce as black trumpet mushrooms, chicory, sweet potatoes, and figs. Steven's brother David runs the logistics of the operation, while distillers Matt Power and Jamie Oakes bring the creative brainstorming and love of the land into delicious beverages. "Matt and Jamie are very passionate outdoors people," says Lee Noble, cocktail director. "Matt has a small farm and is also a biochemist—he's extremely overqualified to do his cool job at Tamworth, haha! Meanwhile Jamie is the forager and the big-picture guy. They're the poets and the science behind what's going on with these interesting liquids we create."

Tamworth has made sure this passion for farming and foraging is reflected in its sourcing: the Hazlet rye in the Chocorua Rye Whiskey comes from Maine, while the Cortland apples in the brandy, the ginger in the ginger vodka, and the berries, black trumpet mushrooms, and maple syrup are all local. This experimentation can also yield some bizarrely intriguing results. For example, the Crab Trapper Whiskey came about from a collaboration with conservationists at the University of New Hampshire as a partial solution to the invasive green crab species destroying indigenous sea life. "We were wondering what to do," Noble says, "and then we thought we could use these crabs as flavoring for whiskey. The end result isn't 'crabby,' but has more of an 'eau de crab' essence from shells and meat, with a little bit of spice that you would put in a crab boil. So we're taking a bite out of this invasive species while making thought-provoking booze."

The fact that Tamworth Distilling keeps its offerings fresh is also what keeps customers coming back to see what's new. And as bars and restaurants up and down the Granite State often feature Tamworth's products in their drinks, their cocktail programs often change as well. "Beyond our core offerings, every year there's something new or experimental coming out," says Noble. "Alcohol is an agricultural product, and that's part of the fun—experimenting with what the land has to offer, and what the market has an appetite for. As we get to do this every day, Tamworth ends up being a kind of test kitchen."

FORAGER'S SMASH

TAMWORTH DISTILLING
15 CLEVELAND HILL ROAD, TAMWORTH

A smash is a classic cocktail, like a julep with fruit," says cocktail director Lee Noble. "This features our ginger vodka made from local ginger, and we talk about how we forage wild strawberries and mint as a tie back to the land. In the end, this is a little semisweet, minty sipper with a kick of ginger."

GLASSWARE: Rocks glass

GARNISH: Mint sprig, strawberry slice

- 2 oz. Common Man White Mountain Ginger Vodka
- 8 large mint leaves
- 6 wild strawberries, or 3 large store-bought strawberries, halved lengthwise
- 1 sugar cube

1. Gently muddle the vodka, mint, berries, and sugar in the bottom of a rocks glass.

2. Fill the glass with ice, and stir until the sugar has completely dissolved.

3. Top off with more ice if necessary.

4. Garnish with a mint sprig and strawberry slice.

WILD HARE

TAMWORTH DISTILLING

15 CLEVELAND HILL ROAD, TAMWORTH

T he base spirit is our aquavit called Skiklubben, which brings out the caraway in this recipe," Noble says. "Aquavit is a unique product with quite a bit of tradition to it. Here, it is the culinary focus, adding spice and herbal flavor to the vegetal and citrus flavors from the fresh-pressed carrot and orange juices."

❧

GLASSWARE: Rocks glass

GARNISH: 4 drops garam masala bitters, dill sprig

- 2 oz. Tamworth Distilling Skiklubben Aquavit
- 1 oz. carrot juice
- 1 oz. freshly squeezed orange juice
- Pinch kosher salt

1. Combine all of the ingredients in a cocktail shaker with ice and shake vigorously.

2. Strain the cocktail into a rocks glass over ice.

3. Garnish with the garam masala bitters and a dill sprig.

RI

THE INDUSTRIOUS SPIRIT COMPANY

1 SIMS AVENUE #103, PROVIDENCE, ISCOSPIRITS.COM

If you follow the Woonasquatucket River west, away from where it drains out into the Providence River, you'll find a neighborhood just outside of downtown that has become a haven for artists and free spirits in recent years. At one point a hub of mills and other factories, the narrow Woonasquatucket lay polluted for decades after these businesses closed, as the area went into postindustrial decline. But starting in the 1990s, the river was cleaned up—so much so that people kayak on it now—and a brownfield was transformed into an indoor farmers market, while the buildings and streets came alive again with arts centers, studios, and collaborative spaces. And where artists go, hip but friendly nightlife is bound to follow. This neighborhood is known as the Valley, and it's the home of The Industrious Spirit Company (ISCO), which was created in its image.

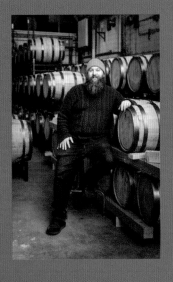

"There are really two threads that run through this business," says Manya Rubinstein, CEO of ISCO. "There's a thread where we promote sustainable farming, and there's the creative production thread, focusing on hands-on making things and collaboration with the creative artist community." As if to carry on the neighborhood tradition of industry and creativity, the distillery is housed in the former site of the Providence Steel and Iron Company, which used to fabricate decorative iron and steel for more than 150 years.

ISCO's genesis was indeed sparked by that moment of two people combining disparate skills and talent to create something bigger. Rubinstein was a New Yorker and a Brown University alumna who had extensive experience in marketing and publishing, but when she settled down in Providence, she found that she was not only loving the close creative connections here, but she also developed a passionate interest in sustainable farming. Meanwhile, her Valley friend Dan Neff had a long background in fermentation and wanted to start a company that reflected how spirits are a perfect expression of agriculture, and he asked for her help with his business proposal.

"The average consumer isn't yet making the connection between what they're drinking and where it comes from," Rubinstein says. "With food, it's cool to know your farmer and what it's made from and how it was raised, but spirits are really far behind with that. This seemed like a neat opportunity to tell some of those stories of climate-smart farming and make something delicious at the same time." The company was incorporated in 2018 and began working on a vodka, with beautifully illustrated labels evoking the city's industrial history, created by Neff's wife, Annaliese. And so Providence's first distillery since Prohibition was born.

When they opened in March 2020, however, the COVID pandemic hit, and like many small distilleries, ISCO made hand sanitizer to help the local community stay healthy and safe. But it also came with an unforeseen upside. "Oh, this was not the start that we envisioned at all, of course," Rubinstein says. "But we do have a big covered outdoor area, so once we were able to reopen, it was one of the few places people could gather outside, with enough space, in a weatherproof area, and hear live music—it became a place of refuge for a lot of people. So our whole business model was turned on its head: we expected to open just a tiny tasting room and basically just distribute our products, but that was reversed." And with a steady stream of business, ISCO was able to take the time to develop its brand in a slower, more organic way.

As for the sustainable-farming thread, ISCO sources most of its organic corn from a partner farm in Hudson, New York, that practices regenerative farming, wherein it focuses on building soil and putting more ground back into the land than it takes out. All the spent grains from the distilling process are then sent to feed pigs and cows in farms around Rhode Island. ISCO sources many of its botanicals from a local group called Sanctuary Farms that works with local immigrant and refugee farmers. For its Blue Velvet Bourbon, ISCO gets blue corn from Clarkson Grain in Illinois, a larger producer, but one that has transitioned to all organic and non-GMO products. "Doing things locally is of first importance," Rubinstein says, "but it's also good to support

larger companies who have decided to go this route. So I'm really interested in working with a local group on the edge of the city and working with a company like Clarkson doing their part, because you need both to get to a better place in terms of climate and farming."

Easily ISCO's most fascinating ingredient, however, is its Ostreida, a corn-neutral spirit distilled with fresh oysters. "Hey, Rhode Island is the Ocean State, and we all love oysters," Rubinstein says. "So we were toasting our survival of our first year in business and wondering how nobody had put a vodka-type spirit and oysters together." Here the "liquor," or brine, from inside the oysters is released into the still as the mollusks steam. As a result, Ostreida has a unique minerality and salinity, combined with a subtle oceanic aroma. Best of all, ISCO features different oysters from different harbors, each with a different "merroir" to the flavor profile, so they note the source on the neck tag of every bottle. And as for the label, it's again by Annaliese Neff, and it evokes the oysters as well as Ursula, the sea witch from *The Little Mermaid*.

Quirky, artistic, and collaborative, with agriculture (or aquaculture) at the core of its identity, this unique spirit is emblematic of the unique creative spirit behind The Industrious Spirit Company. "Here in Providence, everything is DIY and everybody helps everyone else with their projects," Rubinstein says. "It's a much smaller city than New York, so you have to make your own fun. The stakes are different, and you collaborate both by necessity and by the culture of the place. I love that."

PEARL DROP

The Pearl Drop is a variation of the classic Lemon Drop Martini," says Manya Rubinstein, "and it was created to showcase the subtle briny notes present in ISCO's oyster vodka called Ostreida. While Ostreida is often used in savory cocktails like Bloody Marys and Martinis, ISCO developed this drink to illustrate how it pairs with citrus. Meyer lemon and honey add floral notes and richness to this bright beverage, while the herbes de Provence help provide a savory finish."

GLASSWARE: Coupe glass

GARNISH: Lemon twist

- 1½ oz. ISCO Ostreida
- ¾ oz. Honeyed Meyer Lemon Cordial (see recipe)
- ¾ oz. lemon juice
- ½ oz. triple sec
- Herbes de Provence Sugar (see recipe), for the rim

1. Combine all of the ingredients in a shaker tin with ice and shake until chilled and diluted.

2. Strain the cocktail into a coupe rimmed with Herbes de Provence Sugar and garnish with a lemon twist.

continued

HONEYED MEYER LEMON CORDIAL: Combine the zest of 2 Meyer lemons and 4 oz. sugar in a Cambro and let the ingredients macerate overnight. Then, combine the sugar mix, 8 oz. honey, and 12 oz. Meyer lemon juice in a pot over low heat and whisk together until the sugar is fully dissolved. Strain the syrup through a coffee filter, let it cool, then package, label, and date it. Keep the cordial refrigerated.

HERBES DE PROVENCE SUGAR: Grind 2 grams herbes de Provence into a powder, then combine it with 3 oz. superfine (caster) sugar. Mix until incorporated.

SAMARA

THE INDUSTRIOUS SPIRIT COMPANY (ISCO)
I SIMS AVENUE #103, PROVIDENCE

We created the Samara, a Sazerac variation, to highlight the pronounced warm spice notes in Patina, our bourbon barrel aged gin," says Manya Rubinstein. "The syrup adds just enough sweetness and smokiness as an accent, while the Peychaud's bitters and absinthe provide fruity, herbaceous bitterness to balance out the cocktail."

ॐ

GLASSWARE: Rocks glass

GARNISH: Expressed lemon twist

- 2 oz. ISCO Patina Barrel Aged Gin
- ¼ oz. Ancho Maple Syrup (see recipe)

- 4 dashes Peychaud's bitters
- Absinthe, for the rinse

1. Combine all of the ingredients, except the absinthe, in a mixing glass with ice and stir until chilled and diluted.

2. Strain the cocktail neat into a rocks glass rinsed with absinthe and express the oils of a lemon twist over the top and discard.

ANCHO MAPLE SYRUP: Bring 8 oz. water to a boil, then cut the heat and add 1 de-stemmed ancho chile pepper. Let that steep for 20 minutes, then blend it with 8 oz. grade A maple syrup and 4 oz. sugar until the sugar is fully dissolved. Strain the syrup through a fine strainer, let it cool, then package, label, and date it. Keep refrigerated.

NEWPORT CRAFT BREWING + DISTILLING CO.

293 JT CONNELL HIGHWAY, NEWPORT,
NEWPORTCRAFT.COM

These days, when most people think of Newport, they think of expensive yachts, colossal mansions, and quaint streets packed with tourists and party-hardy revelers. Back in Colonial times, this nautical hub may not have boasted the extravagance of today, but the local taste for alcohol was as strong as ever. In fact, with some twenty-two distilleries back then, Newport was known as the Rum Capital of the World. It's a history that is celebrated in every bottle by Newport Craft Brewing and Distilling Co.

Newport Craft was founded as a brewery by four college friends in 1999, but then in 2006, it became the first company in Newport to get a distilling license in 135 years. In 2010, the company finally released its Thomas Tew Single Barrel Rum, named after a seventeenth-century privateer who is so legendary he's also known as the Rhode Island Pirate. The rum was made according to methods from Newport's Colonial heyday, with blackstrap molasses and water fermented in a single copper pot still, then aged in the oak of second-generation American bourbon barrels.

With the growth in beer and rum sales, Newport Craft also physically grew, moving into its current 10,000-square-foot facility, just as it was experimenting with whiskeys. Once they aged for five years or so, the Sea Fog rye and single-malt whiskeys were a revelation, earning 90 and 89 ratings from *Whiskey Advocate*. "It has a higher salinity to it, and we attribute that to our location on the water," explains Newport Craft vice president Ben Chambers. "Rhode Island has great seasonality: much like Kentucky, we get a lot of cold air in the winter and really warm air in the summer, so when it's aging in the barrels, we get great production from our wood, with so much expansion and shrinking of our staves."

In 2017, Newport Craft evolved to the next tier when a group of investors, led by hospitality entrepreneur Brendan O'Connell, bought out the founders. As the new CEO, O'Connell set about expanding production and staff, as well as the national profile of the spirits. In fact, Thomas Tew's name can now be seen on bottles gracing the shelves of more than 500 restaurants and bars, in part because *USA TODAY* has named Newport Craft's flagship as one of the top-ten craft rums in the country. Not only has Thomas Tew been featured at Walt Disney World's EPCOT, but it was also named the official rum of the New York Mets baseball team in 2020.

If all this history sounds glorious, Newport Craft is also aware of the dark side of rum's past. This crucial history is featured as a key part of the facility's latest $20 million expansion project: a multilevel rum museum slated to open early in 2024. Not only does it explore the excitement and the techniques of Newport's fabled distilling history, but also how it was all built on slavery. The first rum was made from fermented sugarcane by slaves in the Caribbean, and the industry was facilitated by the Triangle Trade (see page 13 in the introduction).

"We don't want to look away from this side of the history," Chambers says. "We want to lean into it and pay homage, not just to the people who built the rum industry here in Rhode Island, but the people who made the first rums and what they went through. We're educating people about the history of what we're making and selling, because that's the only way we see how to do it ethically." And to highlight his point, Chambers says that the molasses industry in the United States is still very racially divided, so Newport Craft is looking to source the molasses for its rum from Black-owned farms in the South.

MEET ME AT THE CLIFF WALK

NEWPORT CRAFT BREWING + DISTILLING CO.
293 JT CONNELL HIGHWAY, NEWPORT

The rose hips in this cocktail are an homage to the rose hips found all along Newport's famous Cliff Walk that takes tourists alongside the backyards of the city's seaside mansions. The port wine float, meanwhile, honors the rich Portuguese heritage that is a key part of Newport's seafaring history.

GLASSWARE: Coupe glass

GARNISH: Lemon twist

- 1¼ oz. Newport Craft Sea Fog Rye Whiskey
- 1¼ oz. rose hip syrup
- ¾ oz. egg white
- ½ oz. lemon juice
- Lemon zest, for the rim
- ½ oz. port wine, to float

1. Combine all of the ingredients, except the port wine, in a shaker and shake well.

2. Pour the cocktail into a coupe with a lemon-zested rim. Add a float of the port wine. Garnish with a lemon twist.

THOMAS TEW CANNONBALL PUNCH

NEWPORT CRAFT BREWING + DISTILLING CO.

293 JT CONNELL HIGHWAY, NEWPORT

The infamous Newport privateer Thomas Tew was a scourge for years, until he was killed by a cannonball to the stomach. This cocktail honors him while being gentler on yours.

&

GLASSWARE: Lowball or punch glass

GARNISH: Pineapple wedge

- 1¼ oz. cranberry juice
- 1¼ oz. orange juice
- ¾ oz. Thomas Tew Single Barrel Rum
- ¾ oz. amaretto
- ½ oz. Thomas Tew Widows Walk Rum

1. Combine all of the ingredients in a shaker and shake.

2. Pour the cocktail over ice into a lowball or punch glass and garnish with a pineapple wedge.

VT

CALEDONIA SPIRITS

116 GIN LANE, MONTPELIER,
CALEDONIASPIRITS.COM

Presuming you're ordering cocktails on your sojourns throughout New England, then you're also regularly seeing Barr Hill Gin on the menu. Produced by Caledonia Spirits, Barr Hill is a not a London-style dry gin, but rather an Old Tom gin, which is slightly sweeter. And while you'll certainly notice the juniper in this spectacular spirit, you may wonder at the unusual botanicals that create the complex flavor. You can thank the bees and Vermont's wide range of flora for the raw honey that has been added to the gin.

"We start with a corn-based ethanol, and we use a lot of juniper berry," says Sam Nelis, Caledonia's longtime beverage director, who now goes by the title of "Landcrafted Educator." "We run that once through the still to create a single junipered spirit. When we finish it off with raw honey after the fact, the botanicals in the honey are our botanical blend. That's it. But in that honey, we're expressing those regional botanicals, thanks to 100 to 150 different wildflowers that the bees are foraging."

From the very beginning, Caledonia Spirits has been all about the bees. Todd Hardie had been a beekeeper since he was a boy, and as an adult he was an apiary inspector, helping teach other beekeepers how to keep their insects healthy and stop the spread of disease. He also started making mead and honey wine, but in 2011, he joined forces with Ryan Christiansen, a fermentation expert who owned a homebrewing supply store nearby. Christiansen suggested they make spirits instead, so they opened up their distillery in a 6,000-square-foot barn in Hardwick, up in Vermont's remote Northeast Kingdom, just down the road from the dreamily beautiful Barr Hill Natural Area. Using one fifteen-gallon, direct-fire copper still, they sent their gin out

to competitions and promptly won double gold at the New York International Spirits Competition and Best Gin of the Year in Hong Kong.

From there, word of mouth among bartenders spread the gospel of Barr Hill Gin, and Caledonia Spirits has capitalized on the growth. The company added Tom Cat Gin, aged in American oak barrels for six months, which can be imbibed neat like a whiskey, as well as Barr Hill Vodka, which is distilled entirely from barrels of raw honey. The original gin is still the flagship, accounting for some seventy-five percent of sales, and is now available all around the United States and in countries like Canada, Japan, and the UK. Business was so strong that in 2019 the company moved to a modern 27,000-square-foot distillery in the state capital of Montpelier, and in 2018, Caledonia produced about 30,000 six-bottle cases. Five years later, the company is on track for almost 80,000 cases.

Becoming one of New England's larger distillers hardly means that Caledonia has outgrown its mission of staying true to the land and the bees that pollinate it. For one, Caledonia's headquarters is equipped with environmentally friendly features, from solar panels on the roof, to reclaimed heat from the facility to keep their outdoor patio warm, to using eighty-three percent less water, thanks to reuse. Even more, Caledonia promotes a Bee's Knees Week every fall, a fundraising effort where the company commits to helping plant ten square feet of pollinator habitat each time a bar or restaurant posts a Bee's Knees cocktail on social media. Almost 2,500 businesses nationwide and worldwide have participated, with some 250,000 square feet committed so far. It's just their way of giving back to those precious insects who not only help create wonderful vodka and gin, but also pollinate one-third of all the food we eat.

"We're always trying to connect cocktail culture to agriculture," Nelis says. "When people are drinking a Vodka and Soda at the bar, they're not thinking about how it could be a local product. It's easy to forget that in the spirit world. Distillation is the ultimate form of preservation, and we want people to remember that."

BEE'S KNEES

CALEDONIA SPIRITS

116 GIN LANE, MONTPELIER

This bright, citrus-forward cocktail was created in the 1920s by Frank Meier at the Bar du Ritz in Paris. The makers of Barr Hill consider the Bee's Knees their flagship cocktail, says Caledonia Spirits' Sam Nelis. And indeed, making this classic drink with honey-based Barr Hill Gin is a celebration of our apian pollinators and conservation of their habitat.

&

GLASSWARE: Coupe glass

GARNISH: Lemon twist

- 2 oz. Barr Hill Gin
- ¾ oz. fresh lemon juice
- ¾ oz. honey syrup (2:1)

1. Combine all of the ingredients in a shaker with ice and shake.

2. Strain the cocktail into a coupe and garnish with a lemon twist.

CALEDONIA SPIRITS
GIN
CALEDONIA SPIRITS
RAW HONEY
net wt. 1/2 lb (227g)
HARDWICK, VERMONT

POLLENITA

CALEDONIA SPIRITS

116 GIN LANE, MONTPELIER

This spicy, smoky take on a Margarita was created in 2019 by Nathan Canan-Zucker at Caledonia Spirits.

༄

GLASSWARE: Rocks glass

GARNISH: Fresh rosemary sprig, pinch salt

- Pinch local, fresh rosemary, to smoke
- 1½ oz. grapefruit juice
- 1 oz. Tom Cat Gin
- 1 oz. lime juice
- ¾ oz. local serrano pepper honey
- ½ oz. mezcal espadin
- ½ oz. dry curaçao

1. Torch some rosemary, then place a rocks glass over it to smother the fire and smoke the glass.

2. Combine all of the remaining ingredients in a shaker with ice and shake.

3. Strain the cocktail over fresh ice into the smoked rocks glass.

4. Garnish with a fresh rosemary sprig and a pinch of salt.

VERMONT DISTILLERS

7755 ROUTE 9 EAST, WEST MARLBORO, AND 28 CHURCH
STREET, BURLINGTON, VERMONTDISTILLERS.COM

Dominic Metcalfe recalls how his father, Ed, made hard ciders and fruit wines in the winery attached to their house in Jacksonville, a village in southern Vermont. When Ed founded North River Winery in 1985, it was the only such business licensed in the state. He would package and sell the hard cider as an artisanal product in wine bottles, but by 1997, he was tired of doing it and closed up shop . . . but that was hardly the end.

"My dad is an entrepreneur," Dominic says. "He started the distillery when I turned 21. He established it in 2008, and the first product came out in 2012."

Where the Metcalfes located Vermont Distillers is half the fun: the renovated base lodge at the long-defunct Hogback Mountain Ski Area. Opened for the 1947–1948 ski season, Hogback enticed skiers to southern Vermont with easy access from Vermont Route 9, which stretches from Brattleboro to Bennington. Though it had just a 500-foot vertical drop, it did boast a base elevation of 1,900 feet, which made prospects of decent snow more likely. But over the decades, subpar seasons and increased competition from larger ski areas like Mount Snow caused Hogback to close in 1986. Today it's maintained by a conservation association, with backcountry trails open for hiking and skiing, and with the Metcalfe family offering handcrafted spirits to taste and buy.

"Our tasting room is a special addition to the original building," Dominic says. "But the basement has old posters of old ski areas here and in the Alps—that was where they did ski rentals, and that's where we found all kinds of ski straps and rub-on wax. There were once

horse stalls in our production area. We found an old sticker from the ski area on a window, and we adopted part of it for our logo that we use on a bunch of merchandise."

The difference between Ed's winery back then and his distillery today is that he now runs the business with his adult sons. Dominic's brother, Augustus, helps their father out running the still, gathering the source materials, blending the products, bottling and labeling, and even plowing out the place when the snow falls heavily in winter. Meanwhile, Dominic lives up north in Winooski, just outside of Burlington, where he runs Vermont Distillers' tasting room in the state's largest city. He also handles marketing and promotions, though he likes to go back to West Marlboro and help with production every other week.

And what the Metcalfes produce is a cornucopia of quintessential New England flavor: bourbons flavored with maple and honey. Liqueurs in flavors like maple cream, blueberry, raspberry, and a limited edition cherry. Limoncello made according to a recipe brought over from Italy by immigrant elders generations ago. A French aperitif

called pommeau that combines apple cider with apple brandy. And they also produce clear spirits like their apple moonshine and Catamount Vodka. And all of the ingredients are sourced as locally as possible: syrup from Corse Maple Farm in nearby Whitingham, and apples from Dwight Miller Orchards in Dummerston. Dominic remembers when his dad would ferment apple cider from that same orchard back in the day. "It's kind of cool that after all these years, we came back to them."

And that's what makes these small family-run businesses in New England so vital: the sense that these connections can be maintained, that a quiet but crucial history can be carried forward. And according to Dominic, his dad remains at the center of it all: "Everything goes through him. He does all the alcohol testing, he manages the day-to-day operations as a whole, you name it. He's never going to stop working."

MAPLE BOURBON MILK PUNCH

VERMONT DISTILLERS

7755 ROUTE 9 EAST,
WEST MARLBORO, AND 28 CHURCH STREET,
BURLINGTON

There can perhaps be no more Vermont-flavored cocktail than this one, which combines the state's famed dairy products with Vermont Distillers' maple bourbon and its maple cream liqueur. "We were the first to make the maple cream liqueur commercially for sale," says Dominic Metcalfe. "It's basically alcohol and cream and maple syrup." And in this case, getting back to the basics is so, so sweet.

GLASSWARE: Coupe glass

GARNISH: Freshly grated nutmeg, cinnamon stick

- 1¼ oz. Metcalfe's Vermont Maple Bourbon
- ½ oz. dark rum

- 1 oz. Metcalfe's Vermont Maple Cream Liqueur
- 1 oz. milk or cream
- ⅛ oz. vanilla extract

1. Combine all of the ingredients in a shaker with ice and shake.

2. Strain the cocktail into a coupe and garnish with nutmeg and a cinnamon stick.

THE BLUEBERRY CLUB

VERMONT DISTILLERS

7755 ROUTE 9 EAST,
WEST MARLBORO, AND 28 CHURCH STREET,
BURLINGTON

I n addition its collection of maple spirits, Vermont Distillers excels at working with fruit, and this silky egg-white cocktail uses the Metcalfe family's blueberry liqueur, which has a deep flavor that is only moderately sweet.

GLASSWARE: Nick & Nora glass

GARNISH: Lemon peel

- ¾ oz. Metcalfe's Blueberry Liqueur
- 1½ oz. gin
- ½ oz. lemon juice
- ½ oz. dry vermouth
- 1 egg white

1. Combine all of the ingredients in a cocktail shaker without ice. Shake hard to build the foam.

2. Add ice to the shaker and shake until chilled.

3. Strain the cocktail into a Nick & Nora glass and garnish with a lemon peel.

PHOTO CREDITS

Pages 6, 301, 302, 304, 307 courtesy of Bully Boy Distillers; pages 9, 65, 341, 342, 345, 346 courtesy of Caledonia Spirits; pages 24–25, 26, 28, 30, 34–35, 142, 258–259, 288, 291, 297, 298 by Matthew Reed Baker; pages 37, 38, 41 by Lonnie Newburn, The Boston Shaker; pages 49, 316, 317, 318, 321, 322 courtesy of Quaker City Mercantile; pages 50, 181, 182, 185, 186 courtesy of Omni Mount Washington Resort; pages 52, 216, 219, 221, 223 courtesy of Paul Tabet; pages 55, 99 by Anthony DiBiase; pages 59, 227 by Kane K. Lewis; pages 60, 350, 353, 354 courtesy of Vermont Distillers, Inc.; page 62 by Sophie Fish; pages 70, 74 courtesy of Ordinary; page 79 courtesy of 116 Crown; pages 80, 83, 84 courtesy of BAR; page 87 by Jamie Oakes; page 89 by Jarred Kyser; pages 90, 93 courtesy of Match Restaurant; page 101 courtesy of Vena's Fizz House; page 103 by Jason Rosemeyer, Bramhall Instagram; page 105 by Mat Trogner; page 107 courtesy of Bay View Collection; page 109 by Meghan Werby; page 111 by Jasmine Burne; page 112 by Christopher J. Kemna; page 119 by Steven McCormack; page 120 by Roberto Cibrian Stockbridge; page 125 by Patrick Panageas; pages 126–127 courtesy of The Newbury Boston; page 129 by Steven Rojas; pages 130–131, 133 by Adam DeTour; pages 134, 137 by Cameron Brown; page 138 by Jessica Desforges; page 145 courtesy of Backbar; page 147 by Fátima "Fafá" Langa; page 149 by Roberta Aranha; pages 152, 154 courtesy of Pagu; pages 156, 159 courtesy of Aqua Bar; page 160 courtesy of Crown & Anchor; page 163 by Anna Worgess; page 164 by Darrius Johnson, Visionary Acts; page 167 courtesy of Bistro Zinc; pages 174–175, 177, 178 courtesy of The Common Man; pages 191, 192 by Neal & Paul Young; page 195 courtesy of 815 Cocktails & Provisions; page 196 by Rachael Jones; page 199 by Erika Follansbee/Parker Street Food + Travel; page 201 by Eileen Ryan; pages 206, 211, 212 courtesy of Julia Broome, Kin Southern Table + Bar; page 215 courtesy of Michael Silva, The Dean Bar; page 225 courtesy of Hot Club; page 229 courtesy of White Horse Tavern; pages 230, 233 courtesy of Coast Guard House; page 234 courtesy of Ocean House; page 237 courtesy of Weekapaug Inn; pages 242, 244, 247, 248 by Joey Jones, @photospoke; page 251 by Skip Ladue; page 252 by Emily Morton, The 126; page 255 by Matt Grant; page 257 courtesy of the Woodstock Inn & Resort; pages 262, 264, 265, 267, 268 courtesy of Hartford Flavor Company; pages 270, 272, 275, 276 courtesy of Westford Hill Distillers; pages 279, 281, 282 courtesy of Liquid Riot Bottling Co.; pages 285, 286 courtesy of Sweetgrass Winery & Distillery; pages 292, 294 by Sophie Friedman; page 304 by Dion VanBoekel; pages 308, 309, 310, 313, 314 by Cheshire Media Company; pages 324, 326, 327, 328, 331 by Connor Sumner; page 325 courtesy of The Industrious Spirit Company; page 332 by

ACKNOWLEDGMENTS

Full disclosure: even after decades of working in magazines, this is my first published book, and I can't think of anyone I can thank more than my wife, Clair Pagnano, who has seen me through so much of my journalism career and has been a brilliant source of ideas and honest opinions—including for this project. She is just simply the best. Much love also goes to our children, Giulia and Ian, who are too young to imbibe anything in this book, but who have been such ebullient cheerleaders that their positivity helped me get it over the finish line. I would also like to thank my parents, Leonard and Donna; my sister, Liz; and my mother- and father-in-law, Sandra and Bill, for inspiring me to work hard, and for being there over many years for many a cocktail made in town by professionals or at home by yours truly, a middling amateur.

I would like to thank the good folks at Cider Mill Press, who took a chance on me with this project and had utmost patience with me as I scrambled to produce the myriad moving parts over many months: Buzz Poole, who encouraged my vision for this book and gave me big-picture guidance on how to accomplish it; Jeremy Hauck, who tirelessly worked through all the text and photos, and edited many drafts, thus producing the volume you have in your hands; and Lindy Pokorny, who first asked me to come on board.

Of course, this book would be nothing without the scores of people who contributed their recipes, photos, and deep mixological knowledge. Endless thanks to the owners, managers, and bartenders of all these restaurants, bars, and distilleries that are featured here. All of them were initially cold-called by me, and they all took a leap of faith that this project would come to light. Their constant enthusiasm for making people happy with hospitality and a finely mixed drink was inspiring, and I hope their spirit comes through in these pages. Of special note, I'd like to thank Lonnie Newburn, owner of the erstwhile Boston Shaker in Somerville, Massachusetts, who spent hours walking me through setting up a home bar, and who also gave me guidance through the vastly expanding world of New England distilling.

Finally, I'd like to raise my Negroni up high and toast all the fine establishments throughout New England, whether or not they made it into this book. When you hit the road in this region, finding the right watering hole at cocktail hour is always a highlight of the day. Thousands of people here are dedicated to this task, they work hard at it, and we are all better off for it. Thanks to them, I had confidence and joy in taking on this project and making it happen over many months, and for that I salute them.

Salud, santé, saúde, sláinte, prost, cheers—mrb

ABOUT THE AUTHOR

Matthew Reed Baker has been a magazine writer and editor for more than 25 years. He was the longtime research and arts editor at *Boston* magazine, where he is still a contributing editor and where he has written about the arts, music, food and drink, travel, and current events all over the New England region. Over the years, he has also written for a variety of outlets, including *The Boston Globe Magazine, ForbesLife, National Journal,* and the media-watchdog magazine *Brill's Content.* An avid music collector, amateur photographer, and mediocre pianist, he lives with his wife, two children, and Trout the cat in the Boston area and in Midcoast Maine.

INDEX

—ABOUT CIDER MILL PRESS BOOK PUBLISHERS—

Good ideas ripen with time. From seed to harvest, Cider Mill Press brings fine reading, information, and entertainment together between the covers of its creatively crafted books. Our Cider Mill bears fruit twice a year, publishing a new crop of titles each spring and fall.

"Where Good Books Are Ready for Press"
501 Nelson Place
Nashville, Tennessee 37214
cidermillpress.com

LOWER

CANADA

R. St. Maurice

Quebec

River St. Laurence

St. Johns Ri.

S. Anns

Trois Rivieres

Sertigan

MAINE

St. Croix R.

Montreal L. & T.

L. St. Peter

R. Chaudiere

Massachusetts Bay

Passamacude Bay

R. St. Francis

Kennebec R.

Belfast

Mt. Desert

Manan I.

L. St. Francis

Ft. Chambly

Sagadahock R.

Fort George

Penobscot Bay

St. John

Lake Champlain

Androscoggin R.

Brunswick

Casco B.

YORK

Crown Pt. Ticonderoga

VERMONT

Hudson or Connecticut R.

NEW HAMPSHIRE

Casco

Portland

Wells

Jefferys Ledge

George L.

Otter Cr.

York

Saratoga

Mohawks R.

Walpole

Ports mouth

Piscatague Hr.

Schuyler

Schenectady

Fulham

Salisbury

Newbury

C. Ann

Bennington

Dunstable

C. Cod

Albany

Deerfield

Peterstraum

Salem

St. Georges Bank

Catskill

Hadley

Cambridge

Barnstable Bay

MASSACHUSETTS BAY

Boston

Kingston

Springfield

Chatham

N. Windsor

Enfield

Providence

Sandy P.

Orange

Hartford

Bristol

Plymouth

Nantucket I.

Poughkeepsie

CONNECTICUT

New Haven

RHODE ISL.

Falmouth

Delaware R.

Courtland

Rye

Newport

Marthas Vineyard

Nantucket Shoals

New York

The Sound

Elizabeth I.

Amboy

Hampstead

LONG ISLAND

NEW JERSEY

Trenton

Staton I.

Burlington

Sandy Hook

Chester

New Inlet

Salem

Li. Egg Harbr.

Gr. Egg Harbr.

CANADA

Utawas R.

Montreal L&T

Trois Rivieres

L. St Peter

Serugan

Tennoute R. Kings T.

L. St. Francis

F. St.

John

F. Chambly

S. Francis R.

LAKE ONTARIO

Cataraqui R.

Sorell

Lake Champlain

Crown Pt

Ticonderoga

George L.

VERMONT

Windsor Connecticut R.

NEW HAMPSHIRE

Port

Oswego

Oneyda L.

Saratoga

Mohawks R.

Schuyler

Schenectady

Lansburg

Albany

Catskill

Pulham

Bennington

Walpole

Portsmouth

Saltsbur

Dunstaple

Peters

Cambrid

Hadley

Boston

MASSACHUSETTS

Springfield

Enfield Providen

Brie

Seneka R.

Onondaga

Cayuga

E   W   Y O R K

Kingston

Windsor

Delaware R.

Orange

Esopus

Hartford

CONNECTICUT

Newhaven

Tyoga R.

Muncey

Branch

N.E. Branch

Wyoming

Berwick

Easton

Courtland

Rye

New York

Richd

Hampsted

The Sound

LONG ISLAND

Sunburg

Lewis T.

T as R.

Lancaster

R. Schuylkill

Newtown

Bristol

Delitchem

Amboy

Trenton

Staton I.

Sandy Hook

LVANIA

Susquehanah R.

Carlisle

York

Philadelphia

Chester

New castle

Salem

Burlingtown

New Inlet

Li. Egg Harbr.

Ga. Egg Harbr.

Baltimore

ARY

NEW JERSEY